Learning to Unlearn

A Mindful Journey Towards Happiness

By: David Scott Yglesias

First Edition 2024

11402 NW 41 St, Suite 225

Doral, FL, USA 33178

Copyright © 2024 by Energy Yoga LLC

All rights reserved. No part of this book may be reproduced or transmitted in any form or by any means, electronic or mechanical, including photocopying, recording, or by an information storage and retrieval system - except by a reviewer who may quote brief passages in a review to be printed in a magazine or newspaper - without permission in writing from the publisher.

For any request please contact: **info@energyyoga.com**

DEDICATION

This book is dedicated to all those who have reignited the flame of my spirit during times when life's challenges momentarily dimmed its brightness. Your unwavering support and unconditional love have been my guiding light, even when I struggled to find it within myself.

May 'Learning to Unlearn' serve as a beacon of healing, illuminating the falsehoods that burden us and cause unnecessary pain and suffering in our lives.

If you are reading this, these words are dedicated to you with heartfelt gratitude. May they serve as a guiding torch, illuminating your unique path through life's journey.

A special thank you goes to my wonderful wife, Yenni, for her unwavering support and patience with me, throughout the creation of this book.

With Love & Gratitude,

David Scott Yglesias

TABLE OF CONTENTS

DEDICATION 5

PREFACE 15

Introduction 17

CHAPTER ONE - 21

I AM WHO I AM 21

   The Story of – "The Lion That Grew Up A SHEEP" 22

   The Story of - "building strength through struggle" 25

   The Story of - "The Weaver's Loom" 30

CHAPTER TWO - 35

WHAT YOU SEE IS WHAT YOU GET 35

   The Story of – "The Boogie Man Mojo" 38

   The Story of – "The Two Arrows" 46

   The Story of – "The Tale of Two Villagers" 49

   The Story of – "The Sands of Impermanence: A Mandala's Journey" 52

CHAPTER THREE - 55

EMPTY THE MIND OF THOUGHTS 55

   The Story of – "The Monkey mind" 57

The Story of – "The Two Travelers and the Farmer" 62

CHAPTER FOUR - 65

IF I GET   , I WILL FINALLY BE HAPPY 65

The Story of – "A Man in Search of a Light" 66

The Story of – "The Missing Cows" 69

The Story of – "The Golden Buddha" 74

CHAPTER FIVE - 77

WHOEVER DIES WITH THE MOST TOYS WINS 77

The Story of – "Less is More" 79

CHAPTER SIX - 83

PRACTICE MAKES PERFECT 83

The story of - "Wabi-Sabi: The Beauty of Imperfection" 85

The Story of – "Imperfection is not a barrier, but a bridge to enlightenment" 88

The Story of – "A Path Bloomed from Imperfection" 91

CHAPTER SEVEN - 95

THE STRONG HOLD ON WHEN THE WEAK SURRENDER 95

The Story of - "The Lotus in the Murky Pond" 101

The Story of - "The monkey's Dilemma" 104

CHAPTER EIGHT – 109

YOU CAN JUDGE A BOOK BY IT'S COVER..............................109

   The Story of - "The Cookie Thief"................................. 111

   The Story of – "The Dead Rabbit" 115

CHAPTER NINE -...119

THE HARDER I WORK, THE HAPPIER I WILL BE......................119

   The Story of – "Breaking patterns of suffering" 123

CHAPTER TEN -...129

Do onto others before they do onto you 129

   Story of – "Crystals and Chocolates: A Tale of Friendship and Faith" 132

CHAPTER ELEVEN - 137

EVERYTHING BAD HAPPENS TO ME......................................137

   The Story of - "The Wisdom of the Banyan Tree"........... 140

   The Story of – "We are the sky and not the clouds"........ 142

CHAPTER TWELVE - 147

TAKE THE PATH OF LEAST RESISTANCE................................147

   The Story of - "Bamboo's Rooted Resilience" 149

CHAPTER THIRTEEN - **153**

YOU CAN NEVER HAVE ENOUGH **153**

Morning Gratitude: A Simple Practice with Profound Impact 154

The Story of - "The Simple Life: The Greek Fisherman" ... 155

CHAPTER FORTEEN - **159**

KEEP YOUR EYE ON THE PRIZE **159**

The Story of - "The Lotus Seeker" 160

CHAPTER FIFTEEN - **165**

SOME BONDS ARE TOO STRONG TO BREAK **165**

The Story of - "How to train an elephant" 166

CHAPTER SIXTEEN - **169**

ONLY THE STRONG SURVIVE **169**

The story of - "The Three Psychiatrists" 171

CHAPTER SEVENTEEN - **175**

BEAUTY FADES BUT DUMB IS FOREVER **175**

The Story of - "Thomas Edison and Our Potential" 176

CHAPTER EIGHTTEEN - **179**

IT IS BETTER TO RECEIVE THAN GIVE 179

    The Story of – "The Two Seas" 181

CHAPTER NINETEEN - 185

IF WE DON'T LIKE THE ANSWER, ASK ANOTHER QUESTION 185

CHAPTER TWENTY - 191

THE ONLY WAY TO STOP CHANGE IS TO RESIST IT 191

    The Story of - "Personal Transformation" 192

    The Story of – "The Leaf on the Stream of Consciousness" 194

CHAPTER TWENTY ONE - 197

IT IS NOT MY FAULT 197

    The Story of – "There's a Hole in MY Sidewalk" 199

CHAPTER TWENTY TWO - 203

THE BEATINGS WILL CONTINUE UNTIL MORAL IMPROVES 203

    The Story of – "The Gentle Shall outlast the strong" 205

The Epilogue 211

MINDFULNESS COURSES and YOGA TEACHER TRAINING 215

ABOUT THE AUTHOR 217

PREFACE

Many years ago, I stumbled upon a book that would forever change my perspective: Zen and the Art of Happiness, by Chris Prentiss. It was deceptively simple, yet its wisdom resonated deeply. Whenever life weighed me down, I'd reach for its pages, and like a soothing balm, it lifted my spirit.

Now, as I offer you my work, "Learning to Unlearn", I hope it becomes a beacon of light for you too. If it touches your heart, I humbly ask you to share it with others—let its wisdom ripple through a world that often grapples with shadows. This book is more than ink on paper; it's a compilation of the Dharma Talks—the very essence of my yoga and meditation classes at Energy Yoga & Wellness Center in Miami, Florida. Some are recreations of ancient stories, handed down orally, while others are modern creations, using mindfulness philosophy.

If you ever find yourself in our vibrant city, consider this an open invitation. Come join a class, breathe with us, and let our collective energy envelop you. You might also enjoy booking an Energy Healing Massage Therapy Session with me, to relax and restore. For those who've already shared mat space with me, these stories will feel like old friends—a comforting return to the heart of our center, where beautiful souls gather.

May this book be your compass, guiding you toward inner peace and the light that resides within.

INTRODUCTION

In the vast expanse of human consciousness, there lies a realm where reality and illusion often intertwine, which can lead us astray on our path of happiness. This book, rooted in the timeless principles of yoga and mindfulness, serves as a beacon of light to help guide you back to your conscious path.

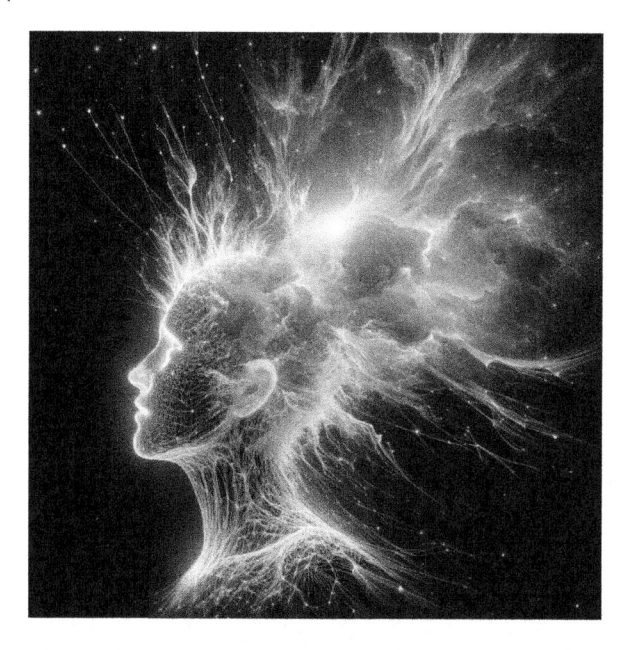

Yoga, an ancient practice, is more than just physical postures. It is a philosophy and science, a way of life that goes beyond the mat. While on the yoga mat, in our practice, yoga teaches us that the highest form of yoga is not the mastery of the physical body, but instead mastery of the mind, using self-observation without judgement. Yoga uses the body as a tool to strengthen the mind.

Eckhart Tolle wisely advised, "Be at least as interested in what goes on inside you as what happens outside. If you get the inside right, the outside will fall into place". As we peel away the illusions of self, they dissolve, vanish, and retreat, much like darkness disperses when illuminated by mindful awareness. In this book, our aim is to assist you in wiping away the emotional dust that has settled on your soul's mirror, allowing you to once again perceive yourself and the world around you, with clarity.

In the ancient book, the Yoga Sutras of Patanjali, in Sutra 1.2 it states: "Yogas citta vritti nirodhah", which can be translated into, "Yoga is the cessation of the fluctuations of the mind". Simply put, the goal of yoga is to learn to control the mind, instead of the mind controlling us.

In our practice we learn that it is often much easier to release our tight hips than in freeing our mind. The least flexible part of the human body is in fact the mind; that is why learning to unlearn is the highest form of learning. If we can discover tools to remove these illusions of truth, our mind can become infinite. The possibilities of what we can evolve into and create will only be limited by our imagination.

As we become the observer, we become aware, and most importantly, gain the ability to unlearn. Unlearning is not about forgetting. It is about letting go of false truths, the illusions that we have accepted as our reality. These illusions, often put in place to protect us or control us, can become barriers to our happiness.

This book is your companion in the process of unlearning. It will challenge your perceptions, question your beliefs, and invite you to view the world from a different perspective. It will guide you to peel back the layers of illusion, one by one, to reveal the true essence of your being.

Remember, the journey to happiness is not about seeking it in the external world, but about realizing it within yourself. The Buddha said that "Learning to unlearn is the highest form of learning". It is not about learning new things, but about unlearning that which is not true. As you turn the pages, may you embark on the most rewarding journey of all - the journey within.

CHAPTER ONE –
I AM WHO I AM

In the quiet corners of our minds, we harbor a belief, an unspoken pact with ourselves, that we are static beings. We accept the labels thrust upon us: "introvert", "artist", "engineer", "failure", "success". These labels, like invisible ink, seep into our consciousness, shaping our self-perception and dictating our choices. But what if we discovered that these labels are mere illusions, flimsy veils obscuring a deeper reality?

"Everybody is a genius. But if you judge a fish by its ability to climb a tree, it will live its whole life believing that it is stupid" - often attributed to Albert Einstein

The Story of – "The Lion That Grew Up A SHEEP"

A pregnant lioness, starving and desperate, roamed the edge of the forest near a meadow. She fell asleep with a roar of grief and hunger, weighed down by the baby lion in her womb. She woke up to the sound of a herd of sheep munching on the grass.

Ignoring the heavy baby lion in her womb, and driven by the frenzy of hunger, the lioness leaped on one of the young sheep and dragged it into the forest. The lioness did not notice that during her wild jump at the sheep she had delivered the baby lion.

The herd of sheep were so terrified by the attack of the lioness that they could not run away. When the lioness had left and the fear had subsided, they were shocked to find the helpless baby lion whimpering among them. One of the sheep mothers felt sorry for the baby lion and adopted it as her own.

The young lion grew up among the sheep acting just like a sheep. The sheep-lion baaed instead of roared and ate grass instead of meat. This herbivorous lion behaved just like a timid, gentle sheep.

One day, another lion came out of the nearby forest onto the green meadow, and to his delight saw this herd of sheep. Excited and hungry, the great lion chased the fleeing herd of sheep, when, to his surprise, he saw a huge lion, with tail up in the air, running as fast as he could ahead of the sheep. Forgetting his hunger, he sprinted and caught the running lion. The sheep-lion collapsed with fear. The big lion was more confused than ever and slapped the sheep-lion to wake him up. In a deep voice he scolded, "What's wrong with you?! Why do you, my brother, run away from me"?

The sheep-lion closed his eyes and baaed in sheep language, "Please spare me. Don't kill me. I'm just a sheep raised with that herd". He grabbed the sheep-lion by the mane with his powerful jaws and pulled him to a lake at the end of the meadow. When the big lion reached the shore of the lake, he pushed the sheep-lion's head so that it was reflected in the water.

The big lion gave the sheep-lion a hard shake. The sheep-lion opened his eyes and was stunned to see that the reflection of his head was not, as he thought, a sheep's head but a lion's head, like that of the lion who was shaking him with his paw. Then the big lion said, "Look at my face and your face reflected in the water. They are the same. My face roars. Now! You must roar instead of baaing!"

The sheep-lion, persuaded, tried to roar, but could only make baa-mixed roars. As the older lion kept urging him with slapping paws, the sheep-lion finally managed to roar. Then both lions jumped across the meadow, entered the forest, and returned to the cave of lions. (The story of a lion that grows up believing it is a sheep is a classic fable often attributed to Sufi poetry)

The story is a great metaphor for all of us who baa with fear and live their whole lives in fears- fears of failure, fears of losing a relationship, fears of anything. You could either live in fear or live with confidence. Either way, you will live but with a huge difference in your quality of life.

You can live cowered in insecurities, or you can live with dazzling self confidence that can move mountains. But don't be in a mask worrying about your future. Don't be a lion with a sheep's soul. That's a waste for both. Not realizing your full potential is like the worst thing you can do to your life (& regret when you get old)! Why would you choose such a life for yourself? Go and express yourself fully.

'A coward dies a thousand times before his death, but the valiant taste of death but once". - William Shakespeare

Shedding Old Skins: suffering

Rewrite Your Narrative and Emerge Anew

We grow up being told that we are born with a fixed set of traits, an unalterable blueprint etched into our very DNA. "You're just like your father", they say, as if our essence is carved in stone. But consider the caterpillar: a humble creature that transforms into a butterfly. Its metamorphosis defies its original form, revealing the latent potential within. The wings of transformation are formed from both patience and struggle. Similarly, we, too, possess the power to shed old skins, rewrite narratives, and emerge anew.

The Story of - "building strength through struggle"

"Transformation can be messy, and it can be beautiful,

but usually it is both". – David Scott

Once upon a time, in a sun-dappled meadow, a delicate butterfly began its miraculous transformation. Within the confines of its chrysalis (similar to a cocoon), it underwent a metamorphosis that would shape its destiny.

The chrysalis, clung to a slender branch, swaying gently in the breeze. The butterfly-to-be was cocooned within, its form obscured by layers of silk. The world outside buzzed with life as birds sang, flowers bloomed, and a boy, curious and kind-hearted, wandered through the grass.

His name was Liam, and he had an affinity for exploring the natural wonders around him. On this warm morning, he stumbled upon the chrysalis, its iridescent surface shimmering like a secret treasure. Liam's eyes widened with wonder. He knew that something magical was about to unfold.

Liam watched as the chrysalis quivered, its walls trembling with anticipation. He imagined the butterfly inside, struggling to break free. Compassion welled up within him. "You're not alone", he whispered. "I'll help you".

From his pocket, Liam withdrew a small knife—a cherished possession passed down from his grandfather. With trembling hands, he delicately sliced through the silk, revealing the butterfly's crumpled form. Its wings, once tightly folded, now lay exposed.

But as the butterfly emerged, something was amiss. Its wings were pale and feeble, lacking the vibrant hues and strength he expected. Instead of soaring into the sky, it crawled along the branch, its movements tentative and uncertain. Liam's heart sank.

"Why can't you fly"? he asked, his voice barely audible. The butterfly's fragile body trembled, and its eyes met Liam's. In that moment, he understood. The struggle, the very act of breaking free, was essential. It was nature's way of building resilience, of forging strength.

Liam sat beside the butterfly, watching as it unfolded its wings. He marvelled at the intricate patterns etched upon them, the delicate veins that carried life. "You need to fight", he urged. "Your wings will gain power through struggle".

Days passed, and Liam tended to the butterfly, trying as best he could to exercise its wings. He offered drops of nectar and whispered encouragement. But still, it could not fly. Its wings remained fragile, and its spirit waned. Liam felt a profound sadness. Had he robbed the butterfly of its destiny?

Then, one morning, as the sun painted the sky with hues of gold, the butterfly stirred. Its wings twitched, and Liam held his breath as he placed it on a branch. Slowly, ever so slowly, it lifted off the branch. The air buoyed it upward, and Liam's heart soared alongside it.

The butterfly circled Liam, its wings growing stronger with each beat. It danced among the flowers, a living kaleidoscope of color. Liam laughed, tears in his eyes. "You did it", he whispered. "Your struggle made you strong".

And so, the butterfly flourished. It soared to great heights, its wings carrying it across meadows and mountains. Liam watched, knowing that life's challenges were like chrysalises, sometimes confining, often painful, but always transformative. All prized accomplishments are difficult before they become easy.

In the quiet moments, he remembered the butterfly's lesson: Strength emerges from struggle. Just as the butterfly's wings gained power through adversity, so did his own spirit. Liam carried this wisdom with him, a reminder that life's hardships were not obstacles but stepping stones toward resilience.

Often in finding and touching our wounds, we find our purpose. During these periods of transformation and metamorphosis, it is as if we lose ourselves and find ourselves at the same time. Maybe we have been on the trail for so long, that we begin to accept that this our destiny. The obstacles in our way become the way and we believe "I am who I am, I am stuck", but this is not quite necessarily so.

Society whispers expectations into our ears, the script we must follow. "Doctors don't dance", they declare, or "Artists can't be practical". We internalize these scripts, fearing deviation. Yet, history teems with rebels who defied their prescribed roles. The mathematician who composed symphonies, the housewife who became an astronaut, they shattered the echo chamber. Our identity need not be an echo, but we have a voice.

Carl Jung wrote, "I am not what happened to me, I am what I choose to become". We are never too old, and it is never too late for us to make lasting changes in our life. We are always at a new starting point. Our past has shaped us, like clay in a potter's hand, but it does not determine our destination. Life is about constantly tinkering and recalibrating. Not everything that is faced can be changed, but nothing can be changed until it is faced.

Life, much like a ship embarking on a transatlantic journey, is a voyage of discovery and purpose. We set sail from our metaphorical New York Harbor, our dreams and aspirations pointing toward distant shores. Our destination is London, a city of opportunity, growth, and fulfillment. But the journey is rarely a straight linear line. It's a dance with the elements, a delicate balance between intention and adaptation.

As our vessel glides across the vast expanse of existence, we encounter headwinds and crosscurrents. The winds of change buffet us, threatening to veer us off course. Yet, it's in these moments that our destiny hinges on the tiniest adjustments—the subtle shifts in our sails, the recalibration of our compass.

Consider the sailor who, instead of fighting the wind, adjusts the angle of the sails. With each tweak, the ship inches closer to its intended path. Similarly, in life, it's the small choices—the daily adjustments—that shape our trajectory. The decision to wake up a little earlier, to read that inspiring book, to extend kindness to a stranger—all these seemingly insignificant actions accumulate like ripples in a vast ocean.

But what if we ignore the winds and currents? What if we sail blindly, oblivious to the forces shaping our journey? The ship, once bound for London, drifts off course. The icy shores of Iceland loom ahead—a stark reminder of the consequences of neglecting our course corrections.

Our destiny, too, hinges on acknowledging the winds of circumstance—the unexpected setbacks, the serendipitous encounters, the storms that test our resolve. These are not deviations; they are invitations to recalibrate. Perhaps a missed opportunity leads us to a better one. Maybe a detour reveals hidden treasures along the way.

Recalibration isn't about abandoning our dreams; it's about aligning them with reality. It's recognizing that life's currents are as essential as our intentions. We learn to tack against adversity, to trim our sails when necessary, and to navigate by the stars of purpose.

Imagine identity as a compass, not a fixed point. Each decision recalibrates our direction. We choose our affiliations, passions, and pursuits. The student becomes the teacher, the skeptic the believer. The power lies not in the initial coordinates but in the course corrections we make. We can pivot, redefine, and forge new paths. The artist can learn calculus; the engineer can write poetry. The canvas of identity awaits our brushstrokes.

Life whispers, "You are not stuck". The caterpillar knows this secret: transformation is not betrayal; it is evolution. Shed your old skin, embrace uncertainty, and dance with change. The artist can become an engineer; the engineer can find solace in art. The power to reinvent resides within us, waiting for our consent.

Rumi wrote, "I am not this hair, I am not this skin, I am the soul that lives within". The Vedanta, based on the doctrine of the Upanishads, taught that the real purpose of life is the realization of one's own essential nature or "true self". It is to finally realize that you are not that face staring back at you in the morning when you brush your teeth; you are the pure ever-free Atman.

In Hinduism, Atman refers to the true self or the innermost essence of an individual. It is often described as the eternal, unchanging, and ultimate reality that exists beyond the physical body and mind. You are a soul freely exploring Earth in a human form, soak in the experience.

So, dear traveller of existence, discard the myth of fixed identity. You are not a tree rooted in place; you are a river carving its course. Embrace the currents, navigate the bends, and discover the vastness of your own becoming.

The Story of - "The Weaver's Loom"

In a small village nestled amidst emerald rice fields, there lived a weaver named Ram. His nimble fingers danced across the loom, creating intricate patterns on silk and cotton. Ram was content, weaving threads into tapestries that adorned temples and homes. Yet, deep within, a restlessness tugged at his heart—an unspoken longing for something more.

One moonlit night, as the crickets sang their ancient song, Ram sat by the riverbank. The water whispered secrets of distant lands, and the stars painted constellations above. He wondered about the purpose of his existence. Was life merely a series of threads woven together, or was there a grand design waiting to unfold?

In the heart of the forest stood an ancient Bodhi tree, a silent witness to countless seasons and a teacher to the great Buddha himself. Ram decided to seek answers there as the Buddha had once done. He wrapped his loom in a cloth, slung it over his shoulder, and embarked on a pilgrimage.

Days turned into weeks as he walked barefoot through dense forests and rocky trails. His feet blistered, but his determination remained unyielding. Finally, he arrived at the sacred Bodhi tree. Its gnarled roots seemed to anchor it to eternity.

Ram sat cross-legged, his loom beside him. He closed his eyes, seeking solace in silence. Days blurred into weeks, and he fasted, surviving on the nectar of morning dew. His mind churned like the river during monsoon, tossing questions like leaves caught in a whirlwind.

One dawn, as the first rays kissed the Bodhi leaves, Ram heard a rustle. A monk emerged—a serene smile etched on his weathered face. His eyes held galaxies of wisdom. Ram bowed, and the monk gestured for him to sit.

"Ram", the monk said, "you seek recalibration—the fine-tuning of life's loom. Each thread you weave matters. But remember, the loom itself needs alignment".

Ram listened, heart pounding. "How do I recalibrate, revered one"?

The monk leaned closer. "Observe the threads—the choices you make. Are they woven with compassion, kindness, and mindfulness? Or do they fray with anger, greed, and ignorance"?

Ram glanced at his loom. Threads of joy, sorrow, love, and regret crisscrossed, forming patterns he couldn't decipher.

"Every thread", the monk continued, "is a chance to recalibrate. When anger tugs, soften it with forgiveness. When greed pulls, weave generosity. When ignorance clouds, seek wisdom".

Ram nodded. "But what of destiny? Are we mere weavers or part of a cosmic design"?

The monk chuckled. "Destiny is both—threads we inherit and threads we spin. The loom is your vessel, the choices your compass. Adjust the sails, Ram. The winds of karma blow, but you steer".

Ram spent months under the Bodhi tree, unraveling his life's tapestry. He rewove the threads, mending old wounds, stitching purpose into each moment. His loom became an altar—a sacred space where intention met action.

One dawn, as dewdrops clung to leaves, Ram stood before the Bodhi tree. His loom lay at its roots. The monk appeared, eyes twinkling.

"Recalibration is not a grand gesture", the monk said. "It's the whisper of a thread, the tilt of a needle. Today, weave anew".

Ram returned to his village; his loom lighter. He wove compassion into every stitch, gratitude into every knot. The villagers marveled at the vibrancy of his creations—the colors of awakening.

And so, Ram learned that life's recalibration lay not in distant horizons but in the present moment. Each thread, each choice, recalibrated his destiny. The Bodhi tree whispered, "Weave well, dear Ram. Your tapestry touches eternity".

And so, the weaver became a sage, and his loom—a vessel for enlightenment. The river carried his story downstream, where other seekers listened, their hearts echoing the ancient truth: Tiny adjustments today recalibrate our destiny, weaving us closer to the fabric of existence.

CHAPTER TWO –
WHAT YOU SEE IS WHAT YOU GET

In the quietude of our existence, we tread upon the delicate threads of illusion. Our lives, like intricate tapestries, are woven with both threads of truth and mirage. The Buddha, in his profound wisdom, illuminated the path toward discerning reality from illusion—a path that beckons us even today.

In Sanskrit the word "maya" means illusion. Our worlds are kaleidoscopic realms, shimmering with illusions. Maya—the cosmic veil—drapes itself over our senses, obscuring the essence of existence. We mistake the transitory for the eternal, the temporary for the timeless. Yet, beneath this veil lies the truth—the unchanging core of our being.

We dance upon the stage of selfhood, adorned in masks of identity. These masks—crafted by ego, fear, and desire—conceal our authentic nature. We believe ourselves to be separate, isolated entities, forgetting that we are waves in the vast ocean of consciousness. The Buddha whispered, "Anatta"— our ego itself is impermanent. We are not our ego. It is not our true identity; rather, it serves as a misguided guardian, accompanying us on life's journey in an attempt to shield our soul. When we lift the ego's mask, we glimpse our interconnectedness.

Illusion thrives in our attachments. We cling to impermanent treasure: relationships, possessions, accolades, as if they were eternal. Yet, the river of impermanence sweeps them away.

Our lives are like sandcastles built on the shifting sands of time. As the tides change and rise, all our earthly works are washed back out into the cosmic sea of change. We come into this world empty handed and we leave empty handed, in between we tend to the garden of our soul.

During my childhood, whenever someone displayed an overly inflated ego, my father had a gentle way of offering perspective. He would say, 'Remember son, the graveyards are filled with those who believed they were irreplaceable. Stay humble, and you'll find true freedom.'

The Buddha taught detachment, not indifference, but freedom from clinging. In releasing our grip, we discover liberation. In letting go, we are free. Think less, feel more is our mantra.

Within the shadowy corners of our consciousness, fears multiply, unseen yet profoundly felt; fears of loss, of not being enough, of venturing into the unknown. These fears stretch their long shadows, casting doubts on our capabilities. However, wisdom, forged in the hot crucible of life's challenges, lights our way. It teaches us that we can transform our relationship with fear. This wisdom acts as a beacon, piercing through the darkness to reveal that fear itself is a mirage, a mere reflection of our misunderstandings.

We often harbor core beliefs so deeply embedded in our psyche that they color our perception of reality. When faced with evidence that challenges these beliefs, the prospect of embracing this new information can be daunting, if not outright impossible for some. This resistance can lead individuals to cling more tightly to their original convictions, even when they suspect these beliefs might be flawed, in a bid to protect their false sense of self.

This clash between established beliefs and contradictory facts gives rise to 'cognitive dissonance,' a state of mental unease. In an effort to maintain their core beliefs unchallenged, individuals might find themselves rationalizing, ignoring, or even denying any information that disrupts their preconceived notions.

Warren Buffet wisely said "When science proves something we strongly or passionately believe in, to be false, we should write it down immediately, because the human mind will do everything possible to push it out of our memory, (due to cognitive dissonance) and we will forget it in 15 minutes".

Our journey, hard-fought and etched with scars, leads us to insight. We learn to discern the shimmering illusions from the bedrock of truth. A lonely seed planted deep in the dirt must have the faith necessary to rise through the darkness and reach the daylight, to blossom. With each step, we dismantle the myths, revealing the luminous core, the Buddha-nature—within.

Mindfulness becomes our mirror. We gaze into it, observing thoughts, emotions, and sensations. The reflections shift—the ephemeral becomes transparent, the illusory fades. We see the dance of impermanence, and in that seeing, we awaken.

The way you're telling your story to yourself really matters. Your body is listening to everything the mind is telling it. May we tread this path with open hearts, unraveling illusions, and embracing the wisdom that sets us free.

The Story of – "The Boogie Man Mojo"

When my children were little, my youngest, John, was just seven years old. Every night, he faced a formidable adversary: the monsters that lurked in the shadows. As bedtime approached, his wide eyes would scan the room, seeking out imaginary threats. Under the bed, inside the closet—no corner was safe from these nocturnal terrors.

I'd rush to his side, my heart echoing his fear. John would clutch his blanket, trembling, and spill out his worries. "Dad", he'd whisper, "they're out to get me. The monsters. They wait until I close my eyes, and then they pounce".

I'd sit on the edge of his bed, my presence a shield against the unseen. "Don't worry, son", I'd assure him. "I'll stand as a sentinel. No monster will dare cross me and get to you".

But nights turned into weeks, and weeks into months. John's sleep remained restless, haunted by imaginary foes. That's when I decided to tap into the mind's remarkable power—the placebo effect. After all, belief can shape reality, even if that reality is born from a parent's love.

In my yoga practice, I concocted blends of essential oils for relaxation and healing. And so, I set out to create something special for John—a potion that would banish the boogie men once and for all. I chose almond oil as the carrier, infusing it with calming chamomile and soothing lavender. The result: "Boogie Man Mojo"—a label I designed on my computer, complete with mystical fonts and moonlit shadows.

That night, as the moon peeked through the curtains, I anointed John's temples with the elixir. A gentle touch on his third eye, a whispered promise of protection. His eyelids fluttered shut, and for the first time in ages, no cries pierced the darkness. The monsters had retreated, defeated by the magic of a father's love.

Morning arrived, and John's eyes sparkled. "Dad", he grinned, "your potion worked! Not a single monster bothered me last night". And so, our nightly ritual continued—the Boogie Man Mojo ritual. John's room became a sanctuary, guarded by fragrant oils and unwavering belief.

As the seasons changed, John outgrew his fear. The monsters faded into legend, and the Boogie Man Mojo bottle gathered dust. But our collaboration didn't end there. John became my little alchemist, helping me blend oils for my yoga studio. Together, we labeled them "Namaste Oils", infusing each bottle with hope and intention.

Our minds, you see, are potent creators. What we believe shapes our reality. So, let us be mindful of our hopes, for they can manifest as magic—or monsters—depending on where we place our faith.

And that, my friends, is the enchanting tale of Boogie Man Mojo—a potion brewed from love, courage, and the alchemy of a child's imagination.

"What you see is what you get". A simple phrase, yet it carries profound implications. As we delve into the practice of mindfulness, a radiant self-awareness dawns upon us. We begin to recognize that this seemingly straightforward statement is but one of many illusions we've woven into our consciousness—a textile of beliefs that now beckon us to unlearn.

It's been whispered by others, etched into our psyche, and perhaps even wielded as a tool of control or conformity. We've grown accustomed to accepting it as gospel truth, perhaps even resigning ourselves to the role of helpless victims in this grand theater of existence.

Yet, let us pivot. Let us recalibrate our lens of perception. Instead of the rigid maxim, let us embrace a more nuanced truth: "What we project, we perceive to be our reality". The world doesn't unfold before us like an unadorned canvas; rather, it dances through the prism of our own consciousness. Our perceptions are colored by the hues of our experiences—the sweet and the bitter, the luminous and the shadowed.

Consider the lens of our ego—the storyteller that weaves narratives from life's threads. Every encounter, every joy, every heartache leaves its imprint, like dewdrops on a morning leaf. These impressions accumulate, layer upon layer, until our vision becomes veiled by groups. We see not the world as it is, but as we are—through the kaleidoscope of our own history. If you can change the way you look at things, the things you look at will change. In time you can change the person who sees.

Leonardo da Vinci, with his wisdom, once inscribed in his notebook: "All our knowledge has its origins in our perceptions. Assume that your first impression of a problem is biased toward your usual way of thinking". His counsel echoes across centuries, urging us to pivot, to explore alternate angles, to glimpse the problem from fresh vantage points. In this dance of perspectives, clarity emerges.

And then there's Rumi, that mystical poet who wove truth into verses: "This is a subtle truth. Whatever you love, you are". Our affections, our fears—they hold sway over our reality. Love empowers, fear constricts, and our projections shape the very fabric of our existence. What we empower, we manifest.

So, let us sit beneath the Bodhi tree of our own awareness. Let us peel away the layers, unlearn the dogmas, and behold the world anew. For in the dance of projection and perception, we find liberation—the sweet nectar of awakening.

As humans, our limited perception of reality is largely shaped by our five senses: sight, hearing, taste, smell, and touch. However, compared to many animals, our sensory capabilities are somewhat limited.

Sight: Humans have one of nature's most versatile senses of sight, thanks to the four types of photoreceptors in our retina: rods and three different types of cones. This allows us to perceive between 1 and 10 million colors. However, some animals, like the common bluebottle butterfly and the peacock mantis shrimp, have up to 15 and 16 distinct types of photoreceptors respectively. Birds, on the other hand, have superior eyesight to ours, with eagles outperforming us by four or five times in visual acuity.

Hearing: While humans have a decent sense of hearing (between 20 Hz and 20,000 Hz), dogs, for instance, can hear frequencies ranging from 40 Hz to 60,000 Hz. This means dogs can hear sounds at much higher frequencies than humans.

Taste: Dogs also have a different sense of taste. While humans have around 9,000 taste buds, dogs only have about 1,700. However, dogs have a specific taste receptor that humans lack, which allows them to taste water.

Ultraviolet Light Perception: Bees and many other insects can see ultraviolet light, which is invisible to humans. This helps them locate nectar in flowers, as many plant species have patterns on their flowers that can only be seen in ultraviolet light.

Thermal Detection: Snakes, particularly pit vipers, pythons, and boas, have a highly specialized sensory organ known as the pit organ, which allows them to detect infrared radiation from warm bodies up to one meter away. This is something humans and many other animals are incapable of.

While humans possess a well-rounded set of senses facilitating effective interaction with our environment, many animals possess specialized senses offering them unique and often more intricate perceptions of reality.

Contemplate how our world might appear if we possessed access to the full array of sensory tools present in other creatures. Instead, our perception of reality remains confined by the limitations of the input our senses provide to our brains. Understanding this reality fosters openness and flexibility in my thinking, allowing me to acknowledge the vastness of the unknown. It reminds me that there are realms beyond our current understanding, encouraging a more humble and open-minded approach to life. We don't know what we just don't know.

When my sons were little, we resided in the rural expanse of South Florida, nestled within the Redlands. Our Sunday evenings followed a cherished ritual: a pilgrimage to Dairy Queen. There, we treated ourselves to an ice cream while reclining in the bed of my pickup truck, gazing upward at the night sky, engaging in rounds of 'I Spy.'

I am fairly certain that you have played the game 'I Spy' before, but just in case, here is a refresher. When playing the game "I Spy", one participant selects an object within their surroundings and provides a clue to the others. The clue typically starts with the phrase "I spy with my little eye", followed by a description of the chosen object. For example: "I spy with my little eye something green". Or "I spy with my little eye something round".

The other players then take turns guessing which object matches the clue. It's a wonderful way to engage with our environment and enhance our observational skills.

Our struggle with perception lies not in our ability to see, but rather in our capacity to retain what we've witnessed. The lens of our eyes captures every detail, rendering it indelible. Yet our minds often wander, preoccupied with solving nonexistent future problems. These fleeting moments of perception ricochet off the mirror of consciousness, slipping into oblivion.

'I Spy' resurrects our awareness. Suddenly, the world around us sharpens back into focus. Even today, I continue this game, walking my dog along the familiar path. Each day, I seek novelty within the routine—a hidden treasure, a subtle shift. It's not that our eyes fail us; rather, our hearts must learn to feel again.

In our yoga class, we often speak of reconnecting with the inner child within us. At birth, everything is a wondrous adventure; we eagerly explore the world, tasting, touching, and leaving our mark on the canvas of existence.

According to Sigmund Freud, between the ages of 3 and 5, the ego begins to take shape, marking the dawn of our individuality. As we grow, we become increasingly conscious of our thoughts, desires, and actions, giving rise to the ego—a bridge between our primal instincts (id) and societal norms (superego).

I observed this transformation firsthand with my own children, as they ventured into the realm of self-expression and their independence with their first defiant "no". It's a journey towards maturity, yet often, in the process, we leave behind the innocence and pure wonder of our inner child.

In our yoga practice, we endeavor to rekindle that youthful spirit, reigniting a sense of openness to life's boundless beauty. So, let go of inhibitions; dare to color outside the lines, and leave your handprints on the walls of time... It's ok.

The Story of – "The Two Arrows"

The Buddhists say that any time we suffer misfortune, two arrows fly our way. The first arrow (physical pain) is the actual bad event, which can, indeed, cause pain. The second arrow (emotional pain) is the suffering. That's actually optional.

The second arrow represents our reaction to the bad event. Being struck by an arrow is painful. Being struck by a second arrow is even more painful.

In the parable of the arrow, sometimes called the second arrow, you picture yourself walking through a forest. Suddenly, you're hit by an arrow. This causes you great pain. But the archer isn't finished, and you can expect a 2nd arrow to come your way. Can you avoid the second one? That's the arrow of emotional reaction. Dodge the second by consciously choosing mindfulness. It will help you avoid a lot of suffering.

The Buddha explained:

"In life, we can't always control the first arrow. However, the second arrow is our reaction to the first. The second arrow is optional".

Avoid the Second Arrow

So, how do you avoid the second arrow? First, notice the first arrow. When you are in physical pain, allow yourself to feel it. You may notice your arrows in other ways, like frustration, irritation, and physical pain. Next, become aware and notice your emotional reaction. Maybe it is a desire to yell or complain to someone. Maybe you get angry with yourself and turn your emotions inward, feeling like you aren't good enough or that there is something wrong with you.

This is the second arrow. Catch yourself, adding more pain and suffering. Finally, give yourself credit for recognizing and avoiding the second arrow. You are learning a new response. You can free up energy for circumstances you can control. However, you can also always adjust your reaction, even if you can't control what happens to you.

We probably find ourselves dealing with the second arrow of suffering many times during the day. The story is not about denying our initial reaction, but instead having a choice of how to proceed. Over time, being aware of this choice, and refraining from shooting endless second arrows at ourselves, can help free us of much unnecessary suffering.

I am a student of Buddhist philosophy and at its very core is the practice of acceptance. It is deeply rooted in the understanding of the impermanence of life and the inherent suffering that comes with human existence. The Second Noble Truth of Buddhism states that "desire (or craving) is the root of all suffering". This is interpreted as wanting reality to be anything but what it is; in other words, a lack of acceptance.

Acceptance, in this context, is not about passive resignation or complacency, but rather about acknowledging and embracing the reality of the present moment. It's about understanding that life is unpredictable, and that change is the only constant. When we resist change or cling to how things used to be, we create suffering for ourselves. On the other hand, when we accept change and let go of our attachment to the past, we can navigate life's transitions with greater ease and less suffering.

However, acceptance does not mean tolerating intolerable situations or resigning oneself to injustice or harm. Instead, it's about recognizing what is within our power to change and what is not.

Yoga teaches us to change the things in life, which should no longer be tolerated and to endure and accept those things which simply cannot be changed.

In situations where change is possible and necessary, acceptance means acknowledging the reality of the situation and then taking appropriate action. It's about seeing things as they are, not as we wish them to be, and then making choices based on this clear-eyed understanding. In situations where change is not possible, acceptance means finding peace in the midst of uncertainty and learning to live with things as they are.

At times you may find a problem with no apparent solution due to our current limited knowledge of reality. This is where acceptance kicks in and we realize that for now, this is not a problem to be solved, but a truth to be accepted. Wisdom is when we can discern the difference between when to hold on and when to let go.

The Buddhist philosophy of acceptance is a powerful tool for navigating the complexities of life. It teaches us to embrace change, to let go of what we cannot control, and to take action where we can. It's a path to greater peace, understanding, and ultimately, liberation.

If we can change the way we look at things, the things we look at begin to transform. Mindfulness does not change how we see the world, but with practice it changes the person that sees.

(The parable of the second arrow, is credited to the Buddha and is found in the Buddhist scriptures. This teaching is part of the early Buddhist texts, specifically in the Sallatha Sutta found in the Samyutta Nikaya, one of the five collections of the Sutta Pitaka in the Pali Canon.)

The Story of – "The Tale of Two Villagers"

In a small village nestled between the mountains and the sea, lived two women, Ananda and Kali. They shared the same town, breathed the same air, and beheld the same reality. Yet, their perceptions of the world, shaped by their past experiences, were as different as night and day.

Ananda, having experienced love and kindness in her life, saw the world as a place of light, love, and abundance. She saw the sun as a radiant symbol of hope, the mountains as majestic guardians of wisdom, and the sea as an endless source of life and possibilities. She saw the villagers as kind-hearted souls, each with their own unique gifts to offer the world.

On the other hand, Kali, who had faced hardships and loss, perceived the world as a place of darkness, fear, and scarcity. She saw the same sun as a harsh and unrelenting force, the mountains as insurmountable obstacles, and the sea as a vast and terrifying unknown. She saw the villagers as competitors, each out for their own survival.

One day, a wise old monk visited the village. He listened to Ananda's joyful tales and Kali's fearful stories about the same village. The monk smiled and said, "You both live in the same village, yet you see it so differently. This is because we do not see the world as it is, but as you are. Our perceptions are not the truth but are merely reflections of our past experiences and inner state".

He continued, "Ananda, your world of light, love, and abundance is a reflection of the love and kindness you have experienced. Kali, your world of darkness, fear, and scarcity is a reflection of the hardships and loss you have faced. But remember, these are just perceptions. They are not the absolute truth".

The monk then taught them the Buddhist principle of acceptance. "Accept the world as it is, without judgment or resistance. Accept your perceptions, but do not be bound by them. Understand that they are not the truth, but merely lenses through which you view the world. And most importantly, know that you have the power to change your lenses, to change your perceptions, and thereby, to change your world".

From that day forward, Ananda continued to spread love and joy in the village, and Kali, with newfound understanding, began her journey of changing her perceptions, slowly transforming her world of darkness into one of light.

Buddhism teaches us the principle of acceptance, which is about acknowledging and embracing the reality of our lives as they are. It encourages us to accept the things we cannot control, such as the impermanence of life, the inevitability of aging, and the presence of suffering. This acceptance is not a form of resignation or defeat, but rather a profound understanding that allows us to live in harmony with the realities of life.

However, acceptance does not mean that we should tolerate injustice, harm, or any form of negativity that we have the power to change. Buddhism also teaches us about the power of action and the importance of making positive changes in our lives. If there are aspects of our lives that cause harm or hinder our path to enlightenment, we are encouraged to take action to change these circumstances.

For instance, if we are in a toxic relationship or an unfulfilling job, Buddhism encourages us to take steps to change these situations rather than passively accepting them. This could mean having difficult conversations, setting boundaries, relocating, seeking professional help, or making lifestyle changes.

In essence, the Buddhist principle of acceptance is about finding a balance between accepting the things we cannot control and taking action to change the things we can. It's about understanding the difference between these two and having the wisdom to respond appropriately. This delicate balance is key to finding peace and happiness in our lives.

The Story of – "The Sands of Impermanence: A Mandala's Journey"

In the secluded reaches of the Himalayas, within the hallowed walls of a Tibetan monastery, a sacred ritual unfolds, manifesting the profound teachings of Buddhist philosophy and the essence of mindfulness. This tale begins with a group of monks, robed in vibrant hues of maroon and saffron, who embark upon a spiritual journey through the creation of a mandala, a symbolic representation of the universe in stunning detail and color, meticulously crafted from grains of sand.

The process commences with a ceremony, invoking divine blessings and setting the intention for the mandala to be a vessel of healing and enlightenment. The monks, skilled artisans of the spirit, gather around a designated area, their tools in hand—metal funnels called chak-pur, used to precisely guide the sand. The design of the mandala, a closely guarded secret revealed only to those who have dedicated their lives to the path, is laid out in an intricate blueprint, a guide to the cosmic representation they are about to create.

Over the ensuing weeks, the monastery is enveloped in a profound silence, broken only by the gentle rubbing of the chak-pur and the occasional chant, a mantra to focus the mind and infuse the mandala with sacred energy. The monks work with unwavering concentration, blowing grains of colored sand into place with meticulous care, each grain a testament to their devotion and a symbol of the transient nature of life.

The mandala gradually comes to life, an explosion of color and geometric precision, embodying the teachings of the Buddha, the cycle of life, death, and rebirth, and the interconnectedness of all beings. It is a labor of love and a meditation in itself, each monk fully present in the moment, mindful of every breath and every movement.

Upon completion, the monastery awakens with the vibrant energy of the mandala, now a radiant focal point of contemplation and prayer. However, this breathtaking creation is not destined to remain. In a profound celebration of impermanence, the monks gather in a ceremony to dismantle the mandala, a poignant reminder that all things, no matter how beautiful or seemingly permanent, are transient.

With prayers and chants, the sand is swept up, blending the colors into a gray mixture that holds within it the energy and blessings of the mandala. The gathered assembly then proceeds in a procession to the nearest river, where the sand is offered to the flowing waters, symbolizing the return of the material to the natural world and the dispersal of its blessings to all corners of the earth.

This act of creation and destruction serves as a powerful lesson in detachment, impermanence, and the interconnectedness of all things. It teaches that while everything in the physical world will eventually fade, the spiritual lessons and insights gained endure, flowing like the river into the vast ocean of consciousness.

Thus, the monks of the Tibetan monastery continue their cycle of creation and dissolution, an eternal dance with the sands of time, embodying the principles of Buddhist philosophy and mindfulness for all who witness this sacred ritual. Through their art, they impart the wisdom of knowing the beauty of the moment, the impermanence of existence, and the practice of letting go, guiding us all towards a deeper understanding of the true nature of reality.

CHAPTER THREE –
EMPTY THE MIND OF THOUGHTS

In the early days of the Modern Mindfulness movement, numerous instructors advocated a seemingly simple yet elusive approach to meditation: emptying the mind of thoughts. This method, they claimed, was the gateway to achieving stillness, inner peace, and lasting happiness.

My own journey with this practice began with high hopes. I remember those early sessions well sitting in quietude, earnestly attempting to silence the incessant chatter of my mind. Yet, instead of finding peace, I was often swept away by a torrent of thoughts, leaving me feeling defeated and inadequate. Each session seemed only to underscore my perceived failures, pushing the sought-after peace further away.

However, my approach to meditation has since evolved. I now see it as akin to entering a dance: there is no final destination or specific outcome to be achieved. I let my breath be my guide, anchoring me in the present moment. For those just embarking on their meditation journey, here is an effective way to start building a nurturing practice:

Softly close your eyes and turn your focus to your breathing. Observe the sensations of air moving in and out of your body. Your breath reflects your inner state. Ask yourself, what messages is your breath conveying? You might concentrate on the rise and fall of your abdomen, the air's passage through your nostrils, or your chest's expansion and contraction— witnessing the wonder of life pulsating within.

As you delve into this practice, it's natural for your mind to drift. When you catch yourself getting sidetracked, gently acknowledge the interruption without casting judgment and redirect your focus to your breathing. The essence of this practice is fostering a compassionate awareness of the here and now.

In my approach to teaching meditation, I often encourage envisioning thoughts as passersby on a bustling city sidewalk. Imagine yourself walking along this sidewalk, absorbed in the rhythm of your steps. Suddenly, a stranger brushes past you. You briefly make eye contact, acknowledging their presence without stopping or engaging further.

As swiftly as they appeared, they continue on their way, blending back into the crowd until they're out of sight. This fleeting encounter mirrors the practice of meditation, where each thought is recognized but not held onto. We observe them, note their presence, and let them drift away, ensuring they don't disrupt our journey.

With ongoing practice, you'll enhance your awareness of your thoughts, feelings, and physical sensations. Embrace everything that surfaces in your consciousness, allowing it to pass without clinging or resistance. Meditation is an art that flourishes with patience and consistency. Initially, it may seem demanding, but persist, and you'll gradually perceive the profound benefits of heightened mindfulness and mental clarity.

When concluding your meditation, do so with intention. Slowly open your eyes, taking a moment to observe any shifts in your mental or physical state. Carry the mindfulness you've cultivated forward into your day.

The Story of – "The Monkey mind"

In her book, "Wisdom and Compassion (Starting with Yourself), Lama Tsomo described the Buddhist concept of the Monkey Mind, that just never stops.

Once, long ago, a man received a wonderful present from a master: a magical monkey that could do anything the man asked of it. Well, of course he was thrilled! He took the monkey along with him and asked it to do all sorts of useful things.

In no time at all, it would finish each task and come running back for the next order. The man had the monkey build him a palace. In no time at all, the monkey had finished it. Now our friend was really thrilled. What's not to like?

The man went to bed for the night and found out. The monkey kept pestering him like a mosquito, "NOW what do you want me to do? What next"? asked the monkey. The man could never rest, ever! Day and night the monkey hounded him with requests for more work, which would then finish in no time. Then it was back for more.

Exhausted and at his wits' end, the man went back to the master. "Help! You've got to give me a way to deal with this monkey so that it doesn't keep on bothering me day and night! What can you do?!"

The master gave him one curly hair. He instructed, "Have the monkey make the hair go straight". The master demonstrated pulling the hair straight. As soon as he let go, the hair bounced back to its former shape. That was it!

The man took the hair and gave it to the monkey, ordering it to make the hair straight. The monkey sat down, fully focused on the little hair. He pulled it straight. It bounced back. He pulled it again. It bounced back again. So, it went on for several hours.

The man raced to his bed and gratefully passed out.

Modern science has illuminated a crucial insight: while halting the incessant stream of our thoughts is beyond our control, we do hold sway over how we respond to these thoughts, ensuring they don't govern us. The age-old notion of "emptying the mind" has been debunked, revealing it as an outdated belief that needs to be reevaluated and set aside.

In our Yoga Teacher Training, I introduce this concept through a practical exercise. I invite you to try it for yourself. Sit in a comfortable position for meditation and attempt to purge your mind of all thoughts, striving to halt the mental chatter entirely. You'll likely find yourself either doubting your technique or acknowledging the futility of the endeavor. The latter realization is accurate: our minds continue their activity until the moment of physical death.

Dr. Sam Parnia, leading critical care and resuscitation research at NYU Langone School of Medicine, notes that consciousness may persist for approximately two to twenty seconds after both breathing and heartbeat cease. This duration reflects the resilience of the cerebral cortex, responsible for thought and decision-making, in the absence of oxygen.

At this juncture, I hypothesize that our spiritual (causal) body separates from our physical (gross) body. The subtle (pranic or energetic) body acts as a bridge linking our soul to the physical realm. When this connection severs, the soul transitions to a state beyond our current understanding.

Our control over the thoughts that traverse our minds is limited. To illustrate, try this: close your eyes, and whatever you do, avoid thinking about a pink elephant. Invariably, the image of pink elephants dominates the mental landscape for many. This isn't a sign of weakness but a testament to our human nature and how we perceive our environment.

The Buddha's teachings highlight the power of our thoughts: "What you think, you become," and "Nothing is more perilous than unguarded thoughts". Our thoughts lay the foundation of our reality; their management and the actions they inspire are pivotal.

Imagine your thoughts as seeds planted in the fertile soil of your mind. The seeds you nurture and tend to will grow, ultimately defining your reality. Like how a majestic oak starts from a small, unassuming seed, the expansive horizons of our future are carved out by the nuanced streams of thought we engage with today. Mindfulness practice encourages us to act as vigilant caretakers of our mental garden.

In this practice, we learn to discern thoughts by their nature—constructive or destructive. We cultivate our minds by fostering positive thoughts and, like diligent gardeners, weeding out negative ones before they root deeply and become challenging to remove.

Buddhist teachings refer to the "emotional cancers of the mind" as greed, anger, and ignorance—fundamental sources of suffering that obstruct our path to enduring happiness and freedom. To counter these poisons, Buddhism promotes the cultivation of generosity, compassion, and wisdom as purifying antidotes, leading to a cleansed state of mind and genuine contentment.

When a negative thought intrudes, we learn to pay it no heed, allowing it to dissipate as swiftly as it appeared. It's akin to burglars fleeing an empty house upon realizing there's nothing to steal.

This process also extends to the internal dialogue we maintain and our self-perception, whether negative or positive. Our interactions with others mirror our self-relationship. What annoys you about others is often simply a reflection our own internal struggles.

Expanding this idea, we understand that others' treatment of us is not arbitrary but a reflection of how we instruct them to, based on our self-treatment. If we have respect for ourselves, we will be treated with respect. If we value ourselves, others will value us. Our thoughts emit energy that shapes our reality through a reciprocal exchange, where the kindness we see in others mirrors our inner radiance.

This underscores the critical importance of self-relationship in mindfulness practice. The relationship with oneself is the longest and most influential one you'll ever have, profoundly impacting all other relationships.

Happiness, fundamentally an internal pursuit, underscores the essence of self-love. While self-love may initially seem self-centered, it is quite the contrary.

Consider the analogy of emergency oxygen masks on an airplane: securing your mask before assisting others is essential for effective help. This principle mirrors the necessity of self-care—without attending to your well-being first, you cannot adequately care for others.

Self-love is the lamp oil that keeps your light burning brightly. Neglecting self-care diminishes your ability to illuminate the lives of others. By prioritizing your well-being, you enhance your capacity to give, love, and live more fully, ensuring that you and those around you thrive.

The Story of – "The Two Travelers and the Farmer"

A traveler came upon an old farmer hoeing in his field beside the road. Eager to rest his feet, the wanderer hailed the countryman, who seemed happy enough to straighten his back and talk for a moment.

"What sort of people live in the next town"? asked the stranger.

"What were the people like where you've come from"? replied the farmer, answering the question with another question.

"They were a bad lot. Troublemakers all, and lazy too. The most selfish people in the world, and not a one of them is to be trusted. I'm happy to be leaving the scoundrels".

"Is that so"? replied the old farmer. "Well, I'm afraid that you'll find the same sort in the next town.

Disappointed, the traveler trudged on his way, and the farmer returned to his work.

Sometime later another stranger, coming from the same direction, hailed the farmer, and they stopped to talk. "What sort of people live in the next town"? he asked.

"What were the people like where you've come from"? replied the farmer once again.

"They were the best people in the world. Hard working, honest, and friendly. I'm sorry to be leaving them".

"Fear not", said the farmer. "You'll find the same sort in the next town".

To sustain a state of happiness, shift your focus from attempting to restrict or clear your thoughts to nurturing positive ones instead. Envision yourself as both the farmer tending to the fields of your mind and the captain steering the ship of your soul. The most reliable predictor of your future is the nature of the thoughts flourishing within you today.

CHAPTER FOUR –
IF I GET _____ , I WILL FINALLY BE HAPPY

In Yoga we realize that much of our unhappiness comes when we look for external things to fill our perceived emptiness inside us. Rumi wrote, "I have been a seeker and I still am, but I stopped asking the books and the stars. I started listening to the teaching of my Soul". So often we erroneously look outside for answers that we can only find within ourselves.

We falsely believe that is only if we get that dream job, find that perfect partner, get that new car, a golden doodle…. on and on, we will finally be happy. In looking outside for fulfillment, we develop an unquenchable thirst for more.

We get that new Louis Vuitton purse and WOW we feel GREAT…. for a little while…. but it does not last. Like a sugar high, that short term euphoria crashes and before long you are looking for the next external thing to fill that void you feel inside your soul. Meanwhile the credit card bills come in and we end up feeling worse than when we started this cycle.

In the Buddhist texts from the Dhammapada, the Buddha taught "Happiness is not something readymade. It comes from your own actions". It is silly to think that someone else could make you happy or unhappy. What if you could find the source of your happiness within you? What if you needed nothing outside yourself for your happiness?

Mindfulness teaches us, that we should not go in search of love, we should go instead, in search of life, and life will find you the love that you seek.

The Story of – "A Man in Search of a Light"

Once upon a time, there was a man who spent his entire lifetime searching for a light that he believed would bring him happiness. He traveled far and wide, over hills and valleys, through forests and deserts, but the light always seemed just out of reach. He thought that it was just over the next hill or around the next bend in the road. But no matter how far he went, he could never find it.

As he grew older, he became more and more desperate. He knew that his time was running out, and he still hadn't found the light that he had been searching for his entire life. It was only on his death bed, with his last few breaths, that he realized that the light he had been so desperately looking for had been inside him the whole time.

He realized that the light was not something that he could find outside of himself, but rather something that he had to cultivate within himself. He had spent his entire life searching for something that he already had, but he was too blind to see it.

The man's story is a reminder that true happiness comes from within. We don't need to search for happiness outside of ourselves, because it is already within us. We just need to cultivate it and let it shine.

Sure, we can enjoy external things, but the trick is not to become attached to them or make them a condition of our happiness. Everything external has an expiration date: metal rust, expensive things get stolen, things wear out or become out of fashion; in time all these facades of happiness become impermanent.

In my beliefs, any item, described as a "luxury brand" with very actual utilitarian value, compared to similar products, is all for show and not for me. My most successful friends do not need a designer brand to protect their image.

In fact, the concept of "stealth wealth," where wealthy individuals choose not to flaunt their riches through designer brands or luxurious displays, is gaining popularity among the world's richest. For instance, Warren Buffett still resides in the same Omaha house he purchased in 1958 for $31,500. During a publicized lunch meeting with Bill Gates, Buffett took Gates to McDonald's and was seen using coupons to pay.

Bill Gates has been spotted wearing a Casio Duro 200 wristwatch, with a retail price of just $50. This is a surprisingly affordable watch, given his wealth, showcasing his preference for functionality, accuracy, and simplicity over luxury.

The Casio Duro 200 is a quartz diver's watch that is water-resistant up to 200 meters and is known for its durability and reliability. In terms of daily accuracy deviation, the Casio Duro 200, with its quartz movement, is approximately 120% more accurate than a mechanical Rolex, when considering Rolex's maximum deviation of +2 seconds per day compared to the quartz's deviation of ±0.5 seconds per day. The price difference is staggering, as popular models like the Submariner, GMT-Master II, and Daytona can range from about $9,000 to over $40,000 for standard editions.

The underlying reasons for practicing stealth wealth include avoiding unwanted attention, reducing the risk of becoming a target for crime or jealousy, and the desire to live a more grounded and genuine life.

These examples highlight a broader societal shift towards valuing genuine experiences and relationships over material symbols of wealth. The stealth wealth movement reflects a growing awareness of the limitations of conspicuous consumption and a desire for a more authentic and meaningful way of living, even among the very wealthy.

Lao Tzu, in the book the Dao De Jing wrote, "When you realize there is nothing lacking, the whole world belongs to you". In truth we really need very few physical possessions to still be happy.

The people that can least afford it are the ones that usually get sucked into the marketing illusion of luxury goods. Often designer brands are just Band-Aids, protecting a bruised and damaged self-identity. They will do anything to not appear to the world unsuccessful; even if it means going into debt for a lifestyle they cannot afford. For a taste of wealth today they may ruin their finances well into their retirement.

It is ok to own things, but not ok when those things begin to own you. Yoga teaches us that less is more; that the truly wealthy in this world are not the ones with the most, but those that need the least for their happiness.

The Story of – "The Missing Cows"

One day the Buddha was sitting with his monks. A distraught farmer approached. "Monks, have you seen my cows"?

The Buddha said, "No we have not".

The farmer continued, "I am distraught. I have only twelve cows, and now they are gone. How will I survive"?

The Buddha looked at him with compassion and said, "I'm sorry my friend, we have not seen them. You may want to look in the other direction".

After the farmer had gone, the Buddha turned to his monks, looked at them deeply, smiled and said, "Dear ones, do you know how lucky you are? You don't have any cows to lose".

As Dr. Joseph Campbell so eloquently said, "The cave you fear to enter holds the treasure you seek". Inside each of us is already a treasure, but sadly few take the time to look within and discover it. We are too busy looking outside ourselves for validation and acceptance. We often seek approval from others, compare ourselves to others, and try to fit in with the crowd. This can lead to feelings of inadequacy, low self-esteem, and a lack of fulfillment.

Especially in this world of social media. So many people look for their approval in the eyes of others. I have always loved this quote from Anaïs Nin where she says, "She lacks confidence, she craves admiration insatiably. She lives on the reflections of herself in the eyes of others. She does not dare to be herself".

In the Tao Te Ching, there is a wise quote, "Those who know do not speak. Those who speak do not know". We tend to take criticism from people we would normally not even take advice from. From the outside, on their Instagram feed, their lives look so much better than ours, but for the most part this is just a filtered illusion.

Yoga teaches us that it is unimportant what others think of us anyway. It is what we think of ourselves that matters. If you seek everyone's approval the only person for sure you will not please is yourself.

When you see how others treat you as a mirror of their own inner state, not as a judgment of your worth, you will gradually learn to let go of your reactions.

The truth is that we all have something special within us that makes us unique and valuable. It could be a talent, a passion, a personality trait, or a life experience. Whatever it is, it is something that only we possess, and it is something that we should cherish and nurture.

In the Taoist Bible, The Tao Te Ching (also spelled Dao De Jing) or just the Tao, which means the way, it eloquently states, "We shape clay into a pot, but it is the emptiness inside that holds whatever we want".

As we unpack this metaphor:

The Clay and the Pot: Just as a potter molds clay into a vessel, we shape our lives, identities, and creations. We build structures, accumulate knowledge, and pursue ambitions. These are the "pots" we create—the tangible, visible aspects of our existence.

The Emptiness Within: The Tao Te Jing reminds us that it is not the external form alone that matters. The true essence lies within—the emptiness, the space, the silence. A German Proverb says, "Silence is a fence around wisdom". This emptiness symbolizes the unmanifest, the unspoken, and the ineffable. It is the canvas upon which life unfolds.

Utilitarian Value: Consider a finely crafted teapot. Its ornate design, delicate handle, and polished surface may dazzle the eye. But it is the emptiness within—the hollow chamber—that serves its purpose. Without that void, it would be mere decoration. The emptiness allows it to hold warmth, steep tea, and nourish our senses.

The Way (Tao): The Tao Te Jing emphasizes the Tao, which means "the way" or "the path". It is both the source and the destination—the underlying principle that governs all existence. The Tao is formless, yet it gives rise to form. It is the emptiness that animates the clay.

Noninterference and Natural Flow: Like the potter who shapes the clay without imposing excessive force, the Tao Te Jing advocates for noninterference. It encourages us to align with the natural flow of life, to embrace simplicity, and to find strength in yielding. In emptiness, we discover fullness. In the Dao it is written, "Whatever is fluid, soft, and yielding will overcome whatever is rigid and hard. What is soft is strong".

In summary, the Tao Te Jing invites us to recognize the value of emptiness—the quietude, the space between thoughts, and the uncarved block. It teaches us that true utility lies not only in what we create but also in what we leave uncreated. As we sip from our teacups, let us remember that it is the emptiness within that gives them purpose, just as the Tao infuses life with meaning.

Mark Twain wrote, "The two most important days in a human's life is the day you are born and the day you find out why". To discover the treasure within us, we need to take the time to look within ourselves. We need to reflect on our lives, our experiences, and our values. We need to identify our strengths and weaknesses, our passions and interests, and our goals and aspirations.

The treasure within us is tempered by the obstacles we overcome. The challenges we face give our life purpose and overcoming them give our life meaning. Just as gold is purified with heat, our soul is purified by the trials we overcome. By doing so, we can gain a deeper understanding of ourselves and our place in the world.

Greatness in life is never birthed without significant pressure and friction. Just as a diamond requires immense friction to be polished, so do life's challenges shape and refine us. These challenges can either erode our essence or reveal our inner brilliance. When you discover the diamond within, you understand your unbreakable nature.

Once we have discovered the treasure within us, we need to share it with the world. We need to use our talents and passions to make a positive impact on others. We need to be true to ourselves and live our lives with purpose and meaning. By doing so, we can inspire others to do the same and create a better world for all.

Life should be a great adventure of rediscovering ourselves. T.S. Eliot wrote, "We shall not cease from exploration, and the end of all our exploring, will be to arrive where we started, and know the place for the first time".

What the study of mindfulness teaches us, is that everything we experience has a profound impact on our self-discovery and knowledge of self. Some people find an impediment in their path and stop there accepting it and not growing. Others find a way over or around the obstacle and expand their consciousness. What we find when we get to the top of an emotional mountain that we have been climbing, is that it never was the mountain we were trying to conquer, but it was our own fears, doubts, and illusions of limitations.

Even if God could take away all the pain you have experienced in your lifetime, God would also have to take back all the wisdom you have acquired in overcoming these painful encounters.

As Wayne Dyer would often say, "Don't die with the music still in you!" Remember, the treasure within you is waiting to be discovered. Take the time to look inside, and you will find it.

Michelangelo was a genius of the Renaissance, who created some of the most famous sculptures in history, such as David and the Pietà. He had a unique vision of art, based on his Neo-Platonic belief that the ideal form of beauty existed in the mind of God, and that the artist's role was to discover and reveal it.

He saw every block of marble as a potential masterpiece, containing the hidden image of a perfect figure. He once said, "The sculpture is already complete within the marble block, before I start my work. It is already there. I just have to chisel away the superfluous material". He used his skill and intuition to carve away the excess stone, and to free the statue from its prison. He believed that he was not creating, but uncovering, the divine beauty that God had placed in the marble.

I hope this book helps you chip away at your hard exterior and reveal your true nature and inner masterpiece inside each of us. Inside each of us, is a golden Buddha just waiting to be revealed.

The Story of – "The Golden Buddha"

In Bangkok there is a golden statue of the Buddha that is 9'8" tall, weighs 5.5 tons and is worth approximatively 250 million in its gold.

The statue was thought to be built in 1,403 and was revered by Buddhist for many hundreds of years. In 1,757 the Burmese Army was invading Thailand. Facing complete annihilation, the Buddhist monks at the monastery hastily began covering their Golden Buddha with plaster which was painted and inlaid with bits of colored glass, to make it look of little or no value to the invading army. During the invasion all the Buddhist monks were tragically murdered, but the Golden Buddha was left undiscovered.

In 1957 an entire Monastery in Thailand was being relocated by a group of monks. One day they were moving a giant clay Buddha when one of the monks noticed a large crack in the clay. On closer investigation he saw there was a golden light emanating from the crack. The monk used a hammer and a chisel to chip away at the clay exterior until he revealed that the statue was in fact made of solid gold.

In yoga we come to the mat and often ask ourselves… "Who are we really, why am I here and where am I going"? What this story so eloquently explains is that inside each of us, there lives a golden Buddha of light. Our purpose in life is to rediscover our Buddha for ourselves.

What happens over the course of our life is that we pile layer upon layer of clay over our own Golden Buddha. The heaviest layer of clay is of our own doing – it's our own limited thinking, false truths and our unconscious conditioning. The other layers of clay get added on from external influences (parents, schools and teachers, bosses and co-workers, society, the media, the church, government and corporations). Eventually we are so laden with clay that we forget that the Golden Buddha is there all the time.

The secret to finding our Golden Buddha, our higher purpose, lies not in the future, but in our past. All we need to do is start chipping away at the clay and rediscovering those things we were passionate about as we grew up. We reconnect with the things that first brought joy into our lives. We recall the times when we were "in the flow" and time stood still. We chip away at our clay during our practice on the yoga mat. As we get close, that golden light from within us will once again emerge. Imagine a world where every person and every company could return to their natural state, their Golden Buddha. Just imagine.

CHAPTER FIVE –
WHOEVER DIES WITH THE MOST TOYS WINS

"Whoever dies with the most toys wins", is another myth that we need to debunk, if we stand a chance of returning to our state of happiness. Yoga teaches us that less is more.

In today's world, materialism and minimalism are two contrasting lifestyles that have gained popularity. Materialism is the belief that possessions and wealth are the key to happiness, while minimalism is the philosophy of living with less and finding joy in simplicity. While materialism is often associated with consumerism and hoarding, minimalism is often associated with decluttering and living a more sustainable life.

Buddhist minimalist philosophy is still relevant today, as it teaches us to focus on the present moment and find happiness in the simple things in life. In fact, many people are turning to minimalism as a way to escape the stress and anxiety of modern life. By simplifying their lives and reducing their possessions, they are able to find more time for the things that truly matter.

Morgan Freeman, in the movie the Bucket List said, "You know, the ancient Egyptians had a beautiful belief about death. When their souls got to the entrance to heaven, the guards asked two questions. Their answers determined whether they were able to enter or not. 'Have you found joy in your life? Has your life brought joy to others?'" So simple and yet so profound.

Yoga philosophy emphasizes the importance of simplicity and contentment. It teaches us that true happiness comes from within, and that we do not need material possessions to be happy. Studies have shown that children who grow up in poverty are often happier than those who grow up in wealthier families. This is because they learn to find joy in the simple pleasures of life, such as spending time with family and friends.

Researchers at the National Foundation for Educational Research, 2016 asked the English pupils, aged between 10 and 15, whether they agreed, disagreed or were unsure about the statement: "I feel happy about life at the moment".

Researcher Benton said: "Our analysis confirms that if we are interested in the happiness and wellbeing of young people, we need to look beyond how much money they have".

"In particular, growing up in a supportive and safe environment, both within the home and elsewhere, appear to be far more important. Parents making the effort to spend time with their children are a major positive influence on their chances of being happy".

While possessions can bring us joy and comfort, there is a strange paradox with materialism. Over time, our possessions can begin to own us, rather than the other way around. The more we accumulate, the more we become enslaved to our possessions. Instead of bringing us happiness, they become a burden that requires constant maintenance, storage and upkeep. So, it's important to strike a balance between materialism and minimalism and find a lifestyle that works for you.

The Story of – "Less is More"

Once upon a time, there was a wealthy merchant who lived in a grand mansion. He had everything he could ever want, in fact almost two of everything, but he was still unhappy. One day, he decided to visit a wise Buddhist monk to seek guidance.

The monk welcomed him and listened patiently to his problems. The merchant explained that he had everything he could ever want, but he was still unhappy. The monk smiled and said, "I think I know what your problem is. You have too much".

The merchant was taken aback. "What do you mean? You can never have too much", he asked.

The monk replied, "You have so much wealth and possessions that you have lost sight of what is truly important. You have become attached to your material possessions, and this attachment is causing you to suffer".

The merchant was confused. "But how can I be happy if I don't have anything"? he asked.

The monk replied, "Happiness does not come from material possessions. It comes from within. The truly rich are not the ones with the most, but the ones who need the least. If you can learn to let go of your attachment to your possessions, you will find true happiness".

The merchant was skeptical, but he decided to take the monk's advice. He began to give away his possessions to those in need. At first, it was difficult, but as he gave away more and more, he began to feel lighter and happier.

Eventually, the merchant gave away almost everything he owned. He was left with only a few possessions, but he was happier than he had ever been before. He realized that he didn't need all of his possessions to be happy. In fact, he was happier with less.

From that day on, the merchant lived a simple life. He no longer needed to worry about his possessions, and he was free to enjoy the simple things in life. He had found true happiness through minimalism.

Remember, that true lasting happiness does not come from material possessions. It comes from within. So, embrace minimalism and find true happiness in simplicity!

CHAPTER SIX –
PRACTICE MAKES PERFECT

Practice makes us better, but it never makes us perfect. If we practice for perfection, we will simply end in frustration, unhappiness, and eventually lose all hope. This is another untruth that we need to unlearn. Yoga teaches us that perfection does not exist in this universe. Real people are never perfect and perfect people are never real.

Perfection is an ideal that many people strive for, but it is also an illusion that can never be attained. The universe is full of imperfections, from the flaws in natural phenomena to the errors in human endeavors. No matter how hard we try, we can never achieve perfection in anything we do, because there will always be room for improvement, criticism, or change.

Seeking perfection in ourselves or others can only lead to unhappiness, because it sets us up for constant disappointment and frustration. When we expect ourselves to be perfect, we put too much pressure on ourselves and ignore our strengths and achievements. We may also develop low self-esteem, anxiety, depression, or other mental health issues.

Perfectionism has been linked with increased rates of mental health disorders, particularly anxiety, depression, obsessive-compulsive disorder (OCD), and eating disorders, such as anorexia.

When we expect others to be perfect, we become overly critical and judgmental of them, and we may lose sight of their positive qualities and contributions. We may also damage our relationships with them, as they may feel resentful, inadequate, or unappreciated.

The Hope Diamond is one of the most famous and most valuable diamonds in the world, but what makes it truly special is a unique flaw. It contains trace amounts of boron. The boron, a flaw, is what gives the Hope Diamond, it's famous blue color.

Upon glancing in the mirror, our gaze often gravitates toward what we perceive as imperfections. Yet, imagine the profound transformation in our lives if, instead of zeroing in on these flaws, we first acknowledged the radiant light shining from our eyes and the warmth of our smile. How would this shift in perspective alter our daily existence?

In Buddhist monasteries, mirrors are typically nowhere to be found and not used. This is because the focus is on cultivating inner peace and wisdom, rather than on external appearances. By avoiding mirrors, monks are able to avoid becoming attached to their physical appearance and instead focus on their internal intellect.

This practice is in line with the Buddhist philosophy of non-attachment, which emphasizes the importance of letting go of material possessions and desires in order to achieve spiritual enlightenment. By focusing on the internal rather than the external, Buddhist monks are able to cultivate a deeper sense of self-awareness and inner peace.

"Beautiful souls are a lot like stained glass windows in a church. On their own they are beautiful in the light of day, but it is in darkest of night, when that light shines from within them, that their true beauty is revealed". – David Scott

A common condition of people as we get older is presbyopia, which is the gradual loss of your eye's ability to focus on nearby objects. It is almost as if God is saying, enough is enough, stop fixating on your wrinkles and blemishes on the outside and start focusing on how you feel on the inside.

The next time you brush your teeth and look at yourself in the mirror, look in your eyes and see your light first. You will realize that all those imperfections (Wabi Sabi) are just badges of honor; battle scars of all the hard-fought wisdom you have thus far achieved in your lifetime.

The story of - "Wabi-Sabi: The Beauty of Imperfection"

In the quietude of ancient Japan, where cherry blossoms whispered secrets and bamboo swayed in reverence, there existed a profound philosophy known as Wabi-Sabi. It was not merely a concept; it was the very essence of existence, woven into the fabric of tea ceremonies, ink-stained scrolls, and the gnarled bark of ancient trees.

700 years ago, those who sought enlightenment understood that perfection was an illusion—a shimmering mirage that danced on the horizon but could never be grasped. The tea masters, the Buddhist monks, and the nobility—they all embraced this truth. They called it Wabi-Sabi, the celebration of imperfection.

Picture a tranquil tearoom, its tatami mats worn by countless footsteps. Here, time slowed, and the mundane became sacred. A single flower nestled in a weathered bamboo vase spoke volumes. Its petals, slightly bruised, held the wisdom of seasons—the fleeting beauty of life itself. The scroll on the wall bore calligraphy strokes, each one imperfect, yet harmonious. And the patina on the tea bowls—their cracks and chips—told stories of resilience and endurance.

Rikyu, the revered tea master, understood this deeply. His teachings transformed tea ceremonies into portals. As guests sipped matcha, they stepped outside the cacophony of their lives. The world beyond the tearoom faded, leaving only the warmth of the cup, the fragrance of leaves, and the hushed conversations between souls.

In Kyoto's majestic gardens, where moss-covered stones whispered secrets to the wind, Rikyu tested his disciple. The garden, meticulously tended, seemed flawless. Yet, Rikyu reached for a maple branch, its leaves ablaze with autumn fire. He shook it gently, and the auburn leaves descended—a dance of imperfection. They landed on the gravel path, mingling with fallen twigs and moss.

The disciple watched, perplexed. Why disrupt perfection? Rikyu smiled, his eyes crinkling like ancient parchment. "Wabi-Sabi", he murmured. "The magic lies not in flawlessness, but in the dance of impermanence. The leaves fall, the seasons change, and we, too, are part of this eternal rhythm".

And so, in that quiet garden, the young man glimpsed enlightenment. The order of nature was never sterile—it was wild, untamed, and gloriously flawed. Imperfection was not a blemish; it was the heartbeat of existence. The tea master's touch had revealed the hidden truth: nothing was ever perfect, nor permanent.

And as the last leaf settled, the wind carried Rikyu's wisdom across centuries. In the rustle of bamboo leaves and the fading echo of a tea bowl lifted, Wabi-Sabi lived on—a fragile, exquisite reminder that imperfection was the brushstroke that painted life's most profound canvas.

What We Practice We Get Good At

In our yoga practice, we focus on constantly evolving into the best version of ourselves possible. Not chasing perfection, but realizing that whatever we practice, we get good at.

In a Warm Dharma Flow Class (warm vinyasa style with a Buddhist twist) that I love to teach, we use a "Progressive Sequence". We repeat asanas (poses) on one side and then the next side of the body. In the next round, we repeat those same asanas and add to them, progressively getting more challenging for up to four rounds. In doing so, asanas that in the first sequence were quite difficult, appear to get easier.

What we find is that the asanas are not getting easier, in fact we are getting better. This reminds us that whatever we practice in life, good or bad, we get better at. If we practice negativity, in time we can become a completely negative person. If we practice being loving and compassionate, that is what our character will reflect.

The power of our thoughts cannot be overstated, for it is from these thoughts that our words take shape. Our words then crystallize into actions, which, through repetition, evolve into habits. These habits lay the groundwork for our character, defining who we are at our core. Benjamin Franklin insightfully remarked, "It is easier to prevent bad habits than to break them". This underscores the significance of mindfulness in guiding our thoughts positively from the outset, shaping a character that reflects our highest selves.

The Story of – "Imperfection is not a barrier, but a bridge to enlightenment"

One day, a young monk named Shanti came to his master, the Buddha, and asked him a question.

"Master, I have been practicing diligently for many years, but I still feel that I am far from perfect. I see many faults and shortcomings in myself and others, and I often get frustrated and discouraged. How can I overcome this feeling of imperfection and attain enlightenment"?

The Buddha smiled and said, "Shanti, you are not alone in feeling this way. Many people, even those who have practiced for a long time, struggle with the same problem. They think that perfection is something that can be achieved by following certain rules, methods, or standards. They compare themselves and others to these ideals, and they suffer when they fall short. They become attached to their views and opinions, and they reject anything that does not fit their expectations. They lose sight of the true nature of reality, which is impermanent, interdependent, and empty of inherent existence".

"Then what is the solution, Master"? Shanti asked eagerly.

"The solution, Shanti, is to embrace imperfection as a natural and inevitable part of life. Imperfection is not a flaw or a defect, but a sign of diversity and uniqueness. It is a source of beauty and creativity, not of ugliness and dullness. It is a teacher and a friend, not an enemy and a foe. It is a catalyst and a motivator, not a hindrance and a deterrent. It is a challenge and an opportunity, not a problem and a burden".

"How can we embrace imperfection, Master"? Shanti wondered.

"We can embrace imperfection by accepting ourselves and others as we are, with our flaws and limitations, and appreciating our diversity and uniqueness. We can recognize that everyone has their own strengths and weaknesses, talents and challenges, virtues and vices, joys and sorrows".

We can respect and appreciate the differences among us and learn from each other. We can also accept the imperfections of the world and see them as opportunities for compassion and wisdom. We can understand that everything is conditioned by causes and conditions, and nothing is fixed or permanent. We can respond to the changing circumstances with flexibility and adaptability, and not cling to our preferences or aversions".

"What else can we do, Master"? Shanti asked.

"We can also embrace imperfection by focusing on our growth and development, rather than our performance and outcomes. We can realize that perfection is not a destination, but a direction. It is not a state, but a process. It is not a goal, but a journey. We can set realistic and attainable goals, and work towards them with diligence and enthusiasm. We can celebrate our progress and achievements and acknowledge our efforts and contributions. We can also learn from our mistakes and failures and use them as feedback and guidance. We can see them as opportunities for improvement and transformation, and not as reasons for regret and guilt".

"Is that all, Master"? Shanti inquired.

"No, Shanti, there is more. We can also embrace imperfection by cultivating a healthier and happier mindset and enjoying our lives more fully. We can do this by developing positive qualities such as gratitude, generosity, kindness, forgiveness, joy, and peace. We can appreciate the blessings and opportunities that we have and share them with others".

We can be kind and compassionate to ourselves and others and forgive ourselves and others for our shortcomings. We can rejoice in the happiness and success of others, and not be envious or jealous. We can also find peace and contentment in the present moment, and not be anxious or worried about the past or the future. We can enjoy the simple pleasures and joys of life, and not be attached or addicted to the worldly pleasures and distractions. We can also meditate and contemplate on the teachings of the Buddha and realize the true nature of ourselves and reality".

"Thank you, Master, for your wise and compassionate advice. I will try to follow it and embrace imperfection in my life". Said Shanti gratefully.

"You are welcome, Shanti. Remember, imperfection is not a barrier, but a bridge to enlightenment. It is not a curse, but a blessing. It is not a problem, but a solution. It is not a weakness, but a strength. It is not a hell, but a heaven. It is not a darkness, but a light. You need a level of darkness to see the stars". The Buddha concluded with a smile.

Salvador Dali was quoted saying, "Have no fear of perfection -- you'll never reach it". Instead of pursuing perfection, we should embrace imperfection as a natural and inevitable part of life. We should accept ourselves and others as we are, with our flaws and limitations, and appreciate our diversity and uniqueness. We should also focus on our growth and development, rather than our performance and outcomes. We should set realistic and attainable goals, celebrate our progress and achievements, and learn from our mistakes and failures. By doing so, we can cultivate a healthier and happier mindset, and enjoy our lives more fully.

The Story of – "A Path Bloomed from Imperfection"

In the heart of a lush valley nestled a monastery, a serene haven where monks devoted their lives to peace, meditation, and the cultivation of wisdom. Among them was a monk known for his daily task of fetching water from a nearby stream. With two large containers suspended from the ends of a sturdy pole he carried across his shoulders, he made his journey at dawn, greeting the morning sun with a silent nod.

One of the containers was perfectly whole, retaining all the water it was filled with, while the other had several small holes, from which water steadily dripped along the path back to the monastery. Aware of this imperfection, the monk nevertheless persisted in his routine, never once seeking to repair the leaking container.

As the seasons passed, the monk noticed a remarkable transformation along the side of the path where the water leaked. Where once there had been nothing but dry, barren earth, a vibrant strip of wildflowers now bloomed, a riot of colors that mirrored the hues of the morning skies. Bees and butterflies danced among the blossoms, and the air was sweet with fragrance.

The other side of the path, which received no water, remained unchanged, its beauty untapped, potential unfulfilled. The leaking container, in its flaw, had unwittingly given life to a barren stretch, creating beauty where none had existed before.

One day, the container, ashamed of its imperfection, apologized to the monk for its inadequacy and the burden it believed to have imposed. The monk, with a gentle smile, shared a wisdom as profound as the teachings of Buddha himself. He spoke of how its unique flaws had allowed a trail of beauty to flourish, teaching a valuable lesson: perfection is not a prerequisite for making a positive impact in the world. In its imperfection, the container had accomplished something truly beautiful, nurturing life along its journey.

This story serves as a poignant metaphor, reminding us that beauty and purpose can arise from imperfection. It celebrates the unconventional paths through which kindness and care can manifest, encouraging an embrace of our flaws and imperfections as avenues through which our unique contributions can flow into the world. Like the wildflowers along the monk's path, the impacts of our actions, no matter how small or flawed they may seem, can bloom into something unexpectedly beautiful, enriching the world around us.

CHAPTER SEVEN –
THE STRONG HOLD ON WHEN THE WEAK SURRENDER

In mindfulness we learn that often tremendous strength is required in letting go in life. It is often the weak that end up holding on way too long to bad situations. The older I get, the more I recognize that it is all that I have lost in life, that has set me free to discover new and almost always better adventures. When you find no solution to a problem, it's probably not a problem to be solved, but instead a truth to be accepted.

Here are two examples of learning when to surrender.

Too much invested to give up:

The sun dipped below the horizon, casting long shadows across the room. Sarah sat there, staring at the remnants of her once-promising venture. The startup she had poured her heart and soul into was now a sinking ship. Yet, she clung to it, unable to let go.

Sarah had invested years of her life, countless sleepless nights, and every ounce of her energy into this project. She had convinced herself that quitting would be a betrayal of her past efforts. The more she struggled, the deeper she sank. Having invested so much, held her captive.

We often find ourselves in Sarah's shoes. We persist in relationships, jobs, or endeavours long after they've turned toxic. Why? Because we've invested so much: time, emotions, and resources, that walking away feels like admitting defeat. We'd rather carry the burden of a bad decision than face the uncertainty of starting anew. **Always remember that** just because the war is lost, it does not mean that you must be conquered.

Comfort in Misery:

Alex sat on the worn-out couch, staring at the cracked ceiling. His marriage had become a barren land, devoid of love, touch or connection. Yet, he stayed. The familiarity of their arguments, the predictable silence—it was oddly comforting.

Change appeared as a risk, and Alex feared its unpredictability. He clung to the familiar suffering—the same old fights, the same cold bed—because it was a pain he knew and understood. Surrendering to change meant stepping into the unknown, and that terrified him.

Nothing grows in the shade of the comfort zone. We all have our comfort zones, even when they're uncomfortable. The misery we know feels safer than the uncharted waters of transformation. We are only afraid right now because we only can see what you could lose; but you have no idea of the infinite possibilities of what could be if we just let go. So, we endure, convincing ourselves that this is as good as it gets. But deep down, we hunger for release, for the courage to break free.

They say when God is ready for you to move, He will make your situation uncomfortable. Is this a time in your life to move?

Surrender is not defeat; it's liberation:

The sun rose, painting the sky with hues of hope. Sarah and Alex faced their demons. They shed the weight of bad decisions, stepped out of their comfort zones, and embraced change.

We, too, can learn from their stories. Letting go isn't weakness; it's resilience. No matter how dark the night, the sun will rise again tomorrow. We often need that dark night of the soul in order to truly appreciate the light of a new dawn and a fresh start. The energy we've invested need not bind us forever. Sometimes, surrendering is the path to transformation—the unpredictable, beautiful dance of life.

In the Yoga Sutras of Patanjali, the Niyamas give us five self-observations as part of The Eight Limbs of Yoga. The fifth Niyama is Ishvara

Pranidhana, and it invites us to explore this concept of surrender. Let's explore the essence of Ishvara Pranidhana and its significance.

The term Ishvara Pranidhana consists of two components: Isvara (meaning "Supreme Being", "God", or "Ultimate Reality") and Pranidhana (which translates to "fixing" or "offering"). In essence, Ishvara Pranidhana encourages us to cultivate a deep and trusting relationship with something greater than ourselves—a force beyond our individual existence. This "something greater" need not conform to any specific religious or dogmatic definition of God; it represents the collective consciousness that binds us all together.

Here are two perspectives on how to apply Ishvara Pranidhana to our lives:

Surrender as Strength: Surrendering is not a sign of weakness; rather, it is an act of immense strength. When we surrender, we release our need for control and allow life to unfold naturally. Just like a fish finding the current and going with it, surrendering aligns us with the flow of existence. It requires patience, trust, and the courage to embrace whatever comes our way. In our asana practice, surrendering is perhaps the strongest thing we can do—letting go of resistance, allowing the breath to guide us, and accepting our present state without judgment.

Navigating Life with Awareness: Surrender is not passive resignation; it's an active choice to accept reality as we see it. By practicing Ishvara Pranidhana, we acknowledge that we are part of a larger whole. We offer our actions, thoughts, and intentions to this collective consciousness. Instead of clinging to familiar suffering, we open ourselves to the unpredictability of surrender and change. It's a path to peace and realization—one that requires no effort or pain on our part, yet it challenges our ingrained need for control.

Ishvara Pranidhana invites us to surrender our ego-driven desires, trust the unfolding of life, and recognize our interconnectedness. It's a profound practice that transcends religious boundaries and empowers us to find strength in letting go.

My hope for you is that if there is a situation in your life that needs to be changed, that you find the courage to release what no longer serves you. May you embrace change, even when it terrifies you a little bit.

Often storms appear in your life not to destroy, but to clear a path for something more beautiful coming your way. For in surrender, lies the promise of renewal. With renewal comes hope.

The Story of - "The Lotus in the Murky Pond"

Once upon a time, in a small village nestled amidst mist-covered mountains, there lived a young woman named Sujata. She was known for her unwavering determination and her ability to face life's challenges head-on.

Sujata had been married to a man named Rajiv for several years. Their relationship had started with love and hope, but over time, it turned sour. Rajiv was consumed by jealousy, anger, and resentment. He constantly belittled Sujata, making her doubt her worth. Despite her efforts to salvage the marriage, it became clear that change was not possible. The love they once shared had withered like a neglected flower.

One day, Sujata sought solace at the village temple. She sat by the lotus pond, watching the delicate pink blossoms float on the murky water. The temple priest, an old sage named Bhante, noticed her distress and approached her.

"Sujata", Bhante said gently, "I see the pain in your eyes. Tell me, what weighs heavily on your heart"?

Sujata poured out her story, the bitterness of her marriage, the shattered dreams, and the relentless struggle to fix what was broken. Bhante listened intently, his eyes reflecting compassion.

"Sujata", he said, "sometimes life is like this lotus pond. The lotus blooms in the muddiest waters, yet its petals remain unstained. Strength does not come from doing what you can do, it comes from overcoming what you first thought was impossible. The lotus draws strength from adversity, rising above the murk to greet the sun".

"But Bhante", Sujata interrupted, "what if the water never clears? What if change is impossible"?

Bhante smiled. "Change is inevitable, my dear. But sometimes, it's not the external circumstances that need changing; it's our perception. The lotus doesn't fight the mud; it accepts its surroundings and transforms them into beauty".

He continued, "Sujata, you have the strength to surrender—to let go of what no longer serves you. Just as the lotus releases its roots from the mud, you can release your attachment to a failing marriage. It takes courage to admit that some paths lead to dead ends".

Sujata pondered Bhante's words. She realized that surrender wasn't weakness; it was wisdom. She decided to end her soured relationship with Rajiv, even though it meant facing uncertainty.

As the days passed, Sujata focused on her own growth, gaining confidence. A bird sitting on a tree is never afraid of the branch breaking, because her trust is not in the branch, but in her own wings. Sujata began trusting in her own wings. Always believe in yourself.

She pursued her passion for painting, opening a small art studio. The lotus became her muse—the symbol of resilience and surrender. Her paintings adorned the walls, capturing the delicate balance between acceptance and transformation.

One morning, Sujata woke up to find a single lotus blossom floating in her studio's water bowl. Its petals were pristine, untouched by the murky water. Tears welled up in her eyes as she understood the message—the lotus had bloomed within her heart.

And so, Sujata learned that surrender wasn't defeat; it was liberation. She let go of the failed relationship, allowing space for new beginnings. Her career flourished, and she found peace in the simple act of surrendering to life's currents.

Whenever villagers visited her studio, they marvelled at the lotus paintings. Bhante would smile knowingly, whispering, "Remember, Sujata, the lotus blooms where it's planted".

And so, Sujata's heart became a lotus, a testament to strength, surrender, and the beauty that arises from letting go.

May we all find the courage to surrender when change is not possible, and may our hearts bloom like the lotus, regardless of life's murky waters.

The Story of - "The monkey's Dilemma"

In the heart of South America, Africa, and Asia, a timeless tale unfolds—a lesson that transcends borders and cultures. It is a story of monkeys, gourds, and the delicate balance between desire and freedom.

The Ingenious Trap:

Natives in these distant lands have devised a cunning method to ensnare unsuspecting monkeys. Their tool? A humble gourd, unassuming yet potent. Here's how it works: they carefully bore a hole into the gourd, just large enough for a monkey's hand to slip through. Next, they attach a rope to the gourd, ensuring it becomes anchored. Finally, they place a tempting prize—a nut or a juicy fruit—inside the gourd and position it where curious monkeys are likely to discover it.

The Monkey's Dilemma:

Picture a curious monkey encountering this peculiar gourd. Driven by hunger, it thrusts its hand through the hole, seizing the tantalizing morsel within. But here lies the twist: the monkey's clenched fist, wrapped around the treat, cannot escape. The hole, designed for entry, becomes a prison for the greedy. And the gourd, now burdened with the rope, defies the monkey's attempts to flee.

The Illusion of Possession:

The monkey's predicament seems absurdly simple to resolve. All it must do is release its grip on the bait, and freedom awaits. Yet, blinded by attachment, it clings desperately. The prize—though meagre—becomes its possession, a symbol of ownership. Fearful of loss, the monkey sacrifices liberty for a fleeting pleasure.

The Human Paradox:

As observers, we shake our heads at the monkey's folly. How foolish, we think, to trade freedom for a morsel! But do we not mirror this behaviour? Our traps are subtler, woven from desires, fears, and attachments. The hardest prison to escape from is our mind. We grasp at possessions, relationships, and beliefs, unaware that our clenched fists imprison us. We, too, forfeit freedom for transient gains.

Breaking Free:

Unlike the monkey, we possess awareness. We can recognize our self-imposed traps—the attachments that bind us. Letting go, though seemingly difficult, holds the key to liberation. The treat we cling to—whether material or emotional—often pales in significance compared to the vast expanse of freedom beyond.

The Choice:

So, let us be mindful. When we find ourselves trapped, palms clenched around illusions, we must pause. Is this possession worth our freedom? Can we release the bait and reclaim our true nature? The monkey's dilemma echoes in our hearts, urging us to choose wisely.

Remember: most of life's traps are of our own making. Let us be the ones who release, who transcend, and who soar beyond the gourd's confines.

May this story remind us to unclasp our hands, relinquish what binds us, and embrace the boundless sky of freedom.

The Story of – "Stepping out of the Comfort Zone"

Ancient wisdom teaches us, "A comfort zone is a beautiful place, but nothing ever grows there". To invite the light of growth and wisdom into our lives, we must venture into the places where this light shines the brightest.

Consider the remarkable story of Hedy Lamarr. Despite being one of the most significant inventors of her era, many remain unaware of the profound impact she had by daring to step beyond her comfort zone. Known in the 1930s and 1940s as the epitome of Hollywood glamour, Lamarr was not just the "most beautiful woman in the world" but also a pioneering inventor whose passion for science and engineering left an indelible mark on the world.

During the turmoil of World War II, Lamarr identified a critical issue: German U-boats were jamming American radio signals, rendering U.S. torpedoes ineffective. Collaborating with composer George Antheil, she ingeniously applied principles similar to those of a piano roll to develop a method for shifting communication signals across 88 frequencies, reflective of the 88 keys on a piano. This method of frequency hopping allowed for secure communication between ships or submarines and their torpedoes, bypassing enemy detection.

Their invention, patented in 1942 (U.S. Patent No. 2,292,387), laid the foundations for technologies we now consider essential: Bluetooth, GPS, and Wi-Fi. Lamarr's journey from a celebrated actress to a key figure in technological advancement exemplifies the profound impact of venturing out of one's comfort zone.

Lamarr's story shines as a guiding light, showing us that within each of us lie dormant ideas and inventions, waiting to be awakened by our courage and willingness to explore. As we embark on our own paths of personal and spiritual growth, let us draw inspiration from her example. Let's embrace introspection and the courage needed to face the unknown. By doing so, we open ourselves to transformation, growth, and the realization of our fullest potential.

Let this ethos of exploration and openness permeate our daily practices, encouraging us to grow not just physically, but also mentally and spiritually. Ask yourself, what unique contributions do you have within you, ready to make a difference in the world?

CHAPTER EIGHT –
YOU CAN JUDGE A BOOK BY IT'S COVER

We often perceive the world through a veil of assumptions, casting judgments based on mere appearances, behaviours, and fleeting actions. Yet, what if we could lift this veil and peer into the depths of each soul? What if we could see beyond the surface, recognizing that every being carries their own intricate mosaic of struggles, hopes, and dreams?

When we judge another, we not only tread upon the delicate petals of fairness but also wound our own hearts. Our hasty assessments may label someone as rude, lazy, or irresponsible, yet these labels are but flimsy paper boats adrift on an ocean of ignorance. Beneath the waves lie hidden currents—their personal battles, their silent victories, and the storms they weather.

Consider the lotus flower, emerging from murky waters to bloom in pristine beauty. Similarly, each person harbors their own story—a narrative etched by life's brushstrokes. To judge is to deny them their unique journey, to overlook the symphony of their existence.

And so, let us tread lightly upon the earth, for our judgments ripple outward. When we label another, we may unwittingly wound their spirit, leaving them feeling misunderstood, rejected, or lesser. Yet, in this dance of perception, we also harm ourselves. Our minds, like tightly clenched fists, close off avenues of growth and understanding.

Instead, let us be compassionate travellers. Curiosity becomes our compass, guiding us toward understanding. We seek to unravel the threads of their experiences—to know where they have walked, what storms they have weathered, and what fragile bridges they have crossed. For within their struggles lie the seeds of resilience, waiting to bloom.

People often build walls, not realizing that bridges connect hearts. Loneliness, like a silent fog, settles upon those who isolate themselves. Let us be architects of connection, weaving bridges of empathy and understanding. We honor their strengths, even as we acknowledge their vulnerabilities. In this shared journey, we extend our hands, offering support and kindness. Rumi wrote, "Why struggle to open a door between us when the whole wall is an illusion"? Judgements can form that illusionary wall.

As the lotus rises from the mud, so too can we rise above judgment. Let our hearts be the fertile soil where compassion blooms, and let our actions mirror the kindness we wish to receive. For in treating others with dignity, we honor the divinity within us all.

May our footsteps be gentle, our eyes open, and our hearts boundless.

The Story of - "The Cookie Thief"

In the quietude of an airport terminal, where fluorescent lights hummed and travellers shuffled like restless ghosts, a karmic dance unfolded—a tale woven with threads of impermanence and shared destiny.

Anku, a weary traveller, had just purchased a bottle of water and an overpriced bag of chocolate chip cookies at an airport snack kiosk. She found what she thought was a quiet place of solace to read a new book. Its pages whispered ancient truths, and she lost herself in its ink-stained labyrinth. But fate had other plans. Beside her sat a man—a Bodhisattva in disguise, perhaps—boldly reaching into her bag of cookies and taking one!

Anku's irritation simmered. She counted the minutes, her patience fraying like an old prayer flag in the wind. "If I weren't so kind", she thought, "I'd blacken his eye with this book".

With each stolen cookie, the man mirrored her actions. When only one remained, Anku wondered: Would he break it in half? His smile revealed the answer, as he took the very last cookie and broke it in half and handed one half to her. The universe chuckled.

"How rude", she muttered, snatching her half. But the man's eyes held no offense. Instead, they whispered, "We are all travellers on this karmic flight".

As her flight was announced, Anku gathered her belongings, refusing to glance back at the audacious thief. She boarded the plane, sank into her seat, and reached for her book. But there instead, nestled among her belongings, lay her unopened bag of overpriced cookies—miraculously returned.

Despair washed over her. "If mine are here", she moaned, "the others were his". The truth struck her like a temple bell: she had been the one that was the cookie thief all along.

In that moment, Kumiko glimpsed the interconnectedness of all beings. The man, the cookies, the flight—they were but transient waves in the vast ocean of existence. She closed her eyes, whispered a silent apology, and vowed to savour each cookie, each encounter, as if it were her last.

And so, as the plane ascended, Anku held her half-cookie, its sweetness mingling with regret. Perhaps, just perhaps, the Bodhisattva beside her smiled, knowing that in this shared imperfection, they had exchanged more than cookies—they had touched the heart of compassion.

May we all learn from Anku's flight, for sometimes, the greatest lessons unfold in the simplest acts of kindness. ("The Cookie Thief" is a story often credited to Valerie Cox)

We do not judge the people we love; we judge the people we fear.

In our encounters with others, let us refrain from judgment, for we cannot truly fathom the inner battles they wage or the validity of our own perspective. Each person carries their unique struggle, and they navigate life with the best they possess. Respect, compassion, and acceptance are their due. By embracing understanding over judgment, we contribute to a more harmonious world—for ourselves and all beings.

When we judge, we unveil our own wounds. When we find these triggers, let us be grateful, for they point to where it is within ourselves that we are not truly free. As Rumi wisely observed, "These pains you feel are messengers; listen to them". Our judgments often stem from our insecurities, fears, and unresolved issues. They are mirrors reflecting our inner landscape. Instead of projecting onto others, let us turn inward, seeking healing and self-compassion.

Judgment erects barriers, distancing us from genuine connection. When we label others, we forfeit the chance to learn, grow, and love. An ancient Amish saying advises, "Put yourself in their place, rather than putting them in theirs". Empathy becomes our sextant. We strive to perceive the world through their eyes, appreciating their strengths, acknowledging their struggles, and celebrating their victories.

Our healing journey begins within. Acceptance of our flaws, forgiveness—for ourselves and others—and seeking guidance when needed are steps toward wholeness. Simultaneously, we extend healing to the world. Through kindness, unity, and hope, we sow seeds of positivity and peace.

Remember the words of Paramhansa Yogananda: "Some people try to be tall by cutting off the heads of others". Every judgment reveals an inner wound, urging us to tend to our own healing with compassion and grace.

"At the end of life, we will not be judged by how many diplomas we have received, how much money we have made, how many great things we have done. We will be judged by I was hungry, and you gave me to eat, I was naked and you clothed me, I was homeless and you took me in. Hungry not only for bread - but hungry for love. Naked not only for clothing - but naked for human dignity and respect. Homeless not only for want of a room of bricks - but homeless because of rejection".

- Mother Teresa

The Story of – "The Dead Rabbit"

Once upon a time, in a quiet neighbourhood nestled among the rolling hills, there lived a man named Mr. Jones. His relationship with his next-door neighbours, the Lopez family, was anything but harmonious. The air between their houses crackled with tension, like heat lightning on a hot August night sky.

Mr. Jones owned a loyal Labrador retriever named Toby. This spirited dog had a penchant for escaping from the confines of Mr. Jones's yard. Toby's escapades were legendary—he roamed the streets, chasing after squirrels and bringing home all manner of deceased creatures. Birds, mice, and even the occasional squirrel adorned Mr. Jones's doorstep, presented by Toby as if they were precious gifts.

One fateful Easter, the Lopez family decided to introduce a new member to their household: a big, fluffy white rabbit. Ana, the Lopez daughter, named the rabbit "Fluffy". The rabbit hopped around their yard, blissfully unaware of the drama unfolding next door.

But fate had other plans. Mr. Jones returned home from work one evening to a scene of chaos. There, in Toby's slobbery jaws, lay poor Fluffy—the once lively rabbit now lifeless. Panic surged through Mr. Jones. He imagined the wrath of the Lopez family, their anger seething like a hidden fire.

Desperation gripped him. He couldn't bear the thought of their eternal disdain. So, he did something both bizarre and compassionate. Mr. Jones carried the chewed-up rabbit into his house, gently washed its fur, and blow-dried it until it fluffed up like a cloud. Then, with trembling hands, he returned Fluffy to the cage in the Lopez's backyard, hoping they would believe it had passed away naturally.

Days passed, and the Lopez family mourned their beloved pet. Ana wept, and her parents consoled her. But the strangest twist awaited them. One sunny morning, as the neighbour watered her plants, she approached Mr. Jones.

"Did you hear that Fluffy died"? she asked, her eyes searching his face.

Mr. Jones stumbled over his words. "Um… no, um… what happened"?

The neighbour's expression turned puzzled. "We found him dead in his cage one day", she said. "But here's the truly bizarre part: the day after we buried him, we discovered someone had exhumed Fluffy, given him a bath, and placed him back in the cage. It's as if some unseen hand cared for him beyond death".

Mr. Jones blinked, contemplating the mysterious turn of events. Perhaps, just perhaps, there existed a force greater than human pettiness—a cosmic kindness that transcended fences and grudges. And in that moment, he glimpsed the interconnectedness of all beings, the delicate threads that wove their lives together.

As the sun dipped below the horizon, Mr. Jones and his neighbour stood there, sharing a silent understanding. Maybe, just maybe, compassion could mend fences, even when the world seemed unyielding. And so, in the quiet of that evening, they both marvelled at the strange resurrection of Fluffy, wondering if it was a lesson from the universe itself.

And Toby? Well, he continued his escapades, blissfully unaware of the profound ripples he'd set in motion—one chewed-up rabbit at a time.

CHAPTER NINE –
THE HARDER I WORK, THE HAPPIER I WILL BE

Hard work is necessary for achieving success and fulfilling one's potential. It requires dedication, discipline, and perseverance.

Hard work can help one overcome challenges, learn new skills, and accomplish goals. Hard work can even be rewarding. There is old saying that says, "When you chop your own wood, you warm yourself twice". However, hard work alone is not enough for living a happy and meaningful life. It is also important to find balance in one's work and personal life.

Balance means having enough time and energy for both work and play. It means being able to enjoy the fruits of one's labor, as well as the relationships and hobbies that make life worth living. Balance also means taking care of one's physical, mental, and emotional health. It means avoiding stress, burnout, and exhaustion that can result from overwork.

Finding balance in one's work and personal life is not always easy. It requires setting priorities, managing expectations, and making compromises. It also requires being flexible, adaptable, and resilient. Sometimes, balance may mean saying no to some opportunities, or delegating some tasks, or asking for help. Sometimes, balance may mean taking a break, or changing one's routine, or trying something new.

At the end of life, most elderly people will say that there are many things they wish they had done more of in their lifetime, but working harder in their career was not one of them. In fact, it is not the things they did in life they regret, but the things they never were able to do, because work got in the way. They may regret not spending enough time with their loved ones, or not pursuing their passions, or not exploring the world. They may regret not living authentically, or not expressing themselves, or not making a difference.

Buddhism teaches that the root of suffering is attachment, which is the tendency to cling to things that are impermanent, unsatisfactory, and not-self. This includes attachment to one's work, achievements, possessions, status, and ego. When one is attached to these things, one becomes dependent on them for happiness, and suffers when they change, disappear, or fail to meet one's expectations. Buddhism also teaches that the way to overcome attachment is to develop insight, which is the ability to see things as they really are, without distortion or delusion. Insight helps one realize that everything is interdependent, impermanent, and empty of inherent existence, and that one's true nature is awareness, compassion, and freedom.

The Dalai Lama, when asked what surprised him most about humanity, answered "Man! Because he sacrifices his health in order to make money. Then he sacrifices money to recuperate his health. And then he is so anxious about the future that he does not enjoy the present; the result being that he does not live in the present or the future; he lives as if he is never going to die, and then dies having never really lived".

Yoga helps one achieve balance in one's work and personal life. Philosophically yoga teaches that we should live as if we are going to die tomorrow but learn as if we were going to live forever. We should be open to everything and attached to nothing.

Physically yoga helps by enhancing one's health, vitality, and flexibility, as well as one's concentration, calmness, and clarity. Yoga also helps one cultivate mindfulness, which is the quality of being fully present and aware of one's experience, without judgment or distraction.

I define the present moment as a very special slice of time. Right now, for example, you have never been this old before and yet you will never ever be this young again. In a short time, this will be a long time ago, so let us not waste it.

Mindfulness is the practice of paying attention to the present moment, without judgment, and with curiosity and compassion. It helps us focus on what matters and let go of what does not. By cultivating a positive mindset, mindfulness enables us to appreciate the beauty and richness of life, and to express gratitude and kindness to ourselves and others.

Contrary to the popular belief in "multi-tasking", science has shown that we cannot think of two things at the same time. It is simply impossible.

As the Native Americans wisely said, "When you try to catch two rabbits, you end up catching none" and "Those who have one foot in the canoe, and one foot on the shore, are going to fall into the river". Mindfulness teaches us to concentrate on one thing at a time, and to illuminate it with our awareness.

Mindfulness is a state of 'bare awareness' that can be practiced in any activity, such as breathing, walking, eating, or working. Mindfulness is often associated with Buddhism, but it is also found in many other traditions.

Mindfulness helps one achieve balance in one's work and personal life by helping one cope with stress, emotions, and challenges, as well as enhancing one's creativity, productivity, and happiness. Stress is not what happens to us. Stress is our response to what happens to us. With mindfulness, we learn that our response is one thing that we actually do have power over. Mindfulness also helps one align one's actions with one's values and goals and live authentically and meaningfully.

Part of being human is experiencing dualities. Within each of us lies both strength and weakness; darkness and light; happiness and sadness. The Taoist symbol of yin and yang reminds us that balance is not about having equal amounts of everything, but rather about finding the right proportion and integration of the different elements that make up our lives.

YIN / YANG

Yin and Yang are like two sides of the same coin - one cannot exist without the other.
Yin / Yang become a metaphor for understanding the nature of the universe.

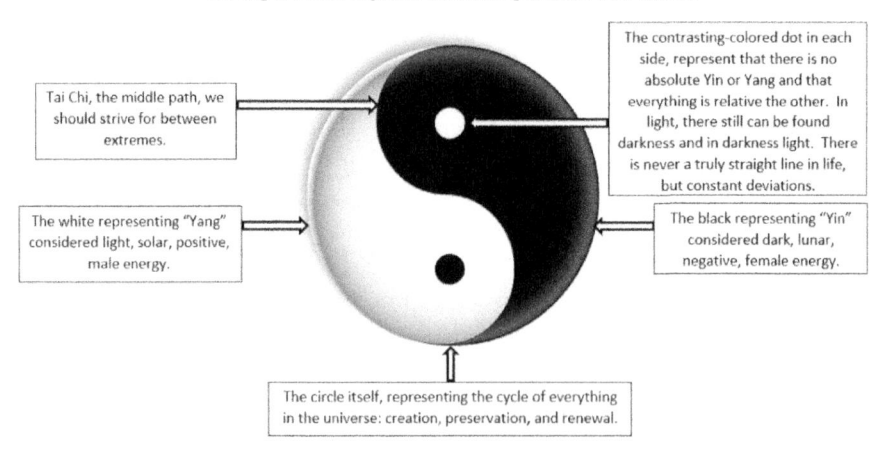

Tai Chi, the middle path, we should strive for between extremes.

The contrasting-colored dot in each side, represent that there is no absolute Yin or Yang and that everything is relative the other. In light, there still can be found darkness and in darkness light. There is never a truly straight line in life, but constant deviations.

The white representing "Yang" considered light, solar, positive, male energy.

The black representing "Yin" considered dark, lunar, negative, female energy.

The circle itself, representing the cycle of everything in the universe: creation, preservation, and renewal.

Yin and Yang represent the complementary and interdependent forces of nature, such as light and dark, hot and cold, active and passive, male and female, and so on. These forces are not opposites, but rather complement each other and create a dynamic equilibrium. Without darkness, it would not be possible to see the stars.

Similarly, in our lives, we need to balance the different dimensions of our well-being, such as our physical, mental, emotional, social, and spiritual health. We also need to balance our work and personal life, which are not separate domains, but rather influence and enrich each other. For example, our work can provide us with a sense of purpose, achievement, and income, while our personal life can offer us love, support, and joy.

However, finding the right balance is not easy, and it may vary depending on our circumstances, preferences, and goals. Sometimes, we may have to prioritize one aspect of our life over another, depending on the situation and the urgency. For instance, we may have to work overtime to meet a deadline, or we may have to take a day off to care for a sick family member. The key is to be flexible and adaptable, and to communicate our needs and expectations with others.

Moreover, finding balance is not a one-time event, but rather a continuous process of self-reflection and adjustment. We need to regularly evaluate how we are spending our time and energy, and whether we are satisfied with the results. We also need to recognize and respect our own limits, and to seek help when we need it. We need to practice self-care and self-compassion, and to appreciate the positive aspects of our lives.

By applying some concepts and practices from Buddhism, yoga, and mindfulness, one can find balance in one's work and personal life and enjoy the benefits of both. One can work hard, but not too hard, and achieve success, but not at the cost of one's happiness. One can also enjoy one's personal life, but not too much, and avoid indulgence, laziness, or escapism. One can find a middle way, a harmony, and a balance, that leads to a fulfilling and satisfying life.

As Brendon Burchard said, "In the end only three things will really matter, did I really live, did I really love and did I really matter"? Therefore, it is wise to find balance in one's work and personal life, while one still can. It is not only beneficial for one's well-being, but also for one's productivity and creativity. It is not only a matter of quantity, but also of quality. It is not only a way of working, but also a way of living.

The Story of – "Breaking patterns of suffering"

There was once a man who had a successful career as a spice trader. He was very ambitious and competitive, and he worked hard to grow his spice empire and earn a lot of money. He was very attached to his work and his reputation, and he thought that they made him happy. He was proud of his achievements and his status, and he looked down on others who were less successful than him.

He carried these emotions with him throughout his life, and they influenced his choices and actions. Not understanding the need for balance, he neglected his family and friends, and often sacrificed his health and well-being for his work. He was happy with his work, but he felt that he was not happy enough. He always wanted more recognition, more money, more power. He was constantly seeking validation and approval from others, but never felt satisfied or fulfilled.

He was unaware that he was creating his own suffering by reliving his deep emotional tendencies, or samskaras. Samskaras are the impressions or imprints that are left in our minds by our past experiences, thoughts, and emotions. They shape our habits, patterns, and reactions, and influence our perception of reality. They are often unconscious, automatic and can be positive or negative. They are a lot like a grinding wheel and can either make us sharp or it can wear us away. Why do we repeat behaviours that constantly dim our lights?

They become like groves on a muddy road. The more often the wagon wheels travel over them, the deeper the grooves get cut in the mud; the harder it is for the wagon wheels to steer out of. The more we repeat these emotional tendencies (samskaras), the deeper they become ingrained in us and the hard they are to break free of.

The man's samskaras were mostly positive, but they caused him to see the world and himself in a distorted way. He was attached to his pleasure and success and identified with them as his true self. He was also averse to anything that challenged or contradicted his views and resisted any change or growth. He was trapped in a cycle of dukkha, the dissatisfaction of life.

One day, he met a woman who was a Buddhist practitioner. She was kind, compassionate, and wise. She saw the man's potential and beauty, and wanted to help him overcome his suffering. She introduced him to the teachings of the Buddha, and explained to him the four noble truths.

The four noble truths of Buddhism are the essence of the Buddha's teachings. They are:

One - The truth of suffering (dukkha): Life involves suffering and impermanence.

Two - The truth of the cause of suffering (samudaya): Suffering is caused by attachments to things, which by their very nature, are impermanent; craving (tanha) for sensual pleasures, existence, or non-existence.

Three - The truth of the end of suffering (nirodha): Suffering can be ceased by detachment; letting go of craving and attaining nirvana, the state of peace and liberation.

Four - The truth of the path that leads to the end of suffering (magga): The way to end suffering is to follow the noble eightfold path, which consists of right view, right intention, right speech, right action, right livelihood, right effort, right mindfulness, and right concentration.

If you follow the Buddha's teachings, she said, you will develop insight, which is the ability to see things as they really are, without distortion or delusion. You will also develop compassion, which is the ability to care for others and yourself, without attachment or aversion. You will then be free from dukkha, and attain the supreme happiness of nirvana.

The man was intrigued by the woman's words. He felt a spark of curiosity and interest, and he asked the woman, "Can you teach me more about the Buddha's teachings? Can you show me the way to overcome dukkha and attain nirvana"?

The woman said, "I can teach you more about the Buddha's teachings, but I cannot show you the way. You have to walk the path yourself, with your own effort and wisdom. You have to see for yourself the truth of dukkha, and the truth of being able to end your suffering. You have to practice the eightfold path and cultivate insight and compassion. You have to realize nirvana and experience the peace and joy that surpasses all understanding".

The man decided to learn more about the Buddha's teachings, and to practice the eightfold path. He also decided to balance his work and personal life, and to share his wealth and happiness with his family, friends, and society. He gradually became less attached to his work and his reputation, and more aware of the impermanence.

He also became more compassionate and generous, and less proud and arrogant. He realized that his true happiness did not depend on external things, but on his own mind and heart. He eventually attained true happiness (nirvana) and became a monk in order to share his bliss with others.

The story illustrates how we attract our own suffering by reliving our deep emotional tendencies, or samskaras. These samskaras are the result of our ignorance and craving, which are the root causes of dukkha. When we are attached to our work, our achievements, our possessions, our status, or our ego, we suffer when they change, disappear, or fail to meet our expectations. We also suffer when we are averse to anything that challenges or contradicts our views, and we resist any change or growth. We are not free, but bound by our own ignorance and craving.

The story also shows how we can overcome our suffering by learning the lesson of the samskaras. The lesson is to see things as they really are, without distortion or delusion. This means to see the impermanence, including in our work, our achievements, our possessions, our status, and our ego. This also means to see the interdependence, compassion, and wisdom of all phenomena, including ourselves and others.

When we see things as they really are, we can let go of our attachment and aversion, and we can cultivate insight and compassion. We can then be free from dukkha, and attain the supreme happiness of nirvana. When we learn the lesson of the samskaras, they dissolve and disappear, and we stop suffering. We experience peace and joy, and we share it with others.

CHAPTER TEN –
DO ONTO OTHERS BEFORE THEY DO ONTO YOU

Honesty, or Satya, is a fundamental principle in the practice of yoga. It is the second of the Yamas, the ethical guidelines outlined in the eight limbs of yoga. Satya encourages us to be truthful in our thoughts, words, and actions. But why is honesty so crucial?

Imagine a yogi sitting in meditation, seeking inner peace and self-awareness. Honesty becomes the foundation upon which this journey rests.

Self-Reflection and Authenticity: When we embrace honesty, we look inward with clarity. We acknowledge our strengths and weaknesses without judgment. Authenticity arises from this self-reflection, allowing us to connect with our true essence. While we can lie to the world, we can never lie to ourselves. We know our truths and we are burdened by the untruths.

Trust in Relationships: Dishonesty erodes trust. Have you noticed how dishonest people often doubt others? Their lack of integrity spills over into their interactions, causing suspicion and strained relationships. In contrast, an honest heart fosters trust and openness.

Yoga does teach us that when given the choice of being kind or in being brutally honest we should choose kindness and prefer silence over expressing anything negative.

Yoga teaches us to choose our words wisely. When we trip and fall, we can almost always get back up. When out of anger we say something hurtful, those words can never be taken back into our mouth. We must live with the words we choose to express our inner feelings.

Alignment with Universal Truth: Satya aligns us with the universal truth. Just as a tree's roots anchor it to the earth, honesty grounds us in reality. When we speak and act with truthfulness, we resonate with the cosmic order, creating harmony within and around us.

Freedom from Guilt: Thich Nhat Hanh wrote, "My actions are my only true belongings. I cannot escape the consequences of my actions. My actions are the ground upon which I stand". Dishonesty weighs heavily on the soul. It creates knots of guilt and anxiety. Honesty, on the other hand, untangles these knots. When we live and act truthfully, our conscience remains clear, allowing us to soar freely.

In his classic book, The Scarlet Letter, Nathaniel Hawthorne wrote, "She did not know the weight, until she felt the freedom". Hester Prynne, the protagonist in the story, has been forced to wear a conspicuous scarlet letter "A" on her chest as a symbol of her sin—bearing a child out of wedlock while her husband was away. The scarlet letter represents her shame, guilt, and societal judgment. For years, it has weighed heavily upon her, both physically and emotionally.

However, when Hester finally removes the scarlet letter, she experiences an unexpected liberation. The burden she carried—the weight of her guilt, shame, public condemnation, and isolation—becomes apparent only when she feels the newfound freedom without it. The scarlet letter had confined her, but its removal allows her to breathe, to feel the wild, unrestrained atmosphere of her own existence.

In this moment, Hester realizes that true freedom lies not in avoiding consequences but in facing them head-on. By shedding the symbol of her guilt, she embraces a different life—one unencumbered by judgment and societal norms. The scarlet letter, once oppressive, becomes a catalyst for her transformation, leading her toward redemption and self-discovery.

When we do something that we know in our hearts is wrong, and we do it anyway, we emotionally wear a scarlet letter of shame and guilt. Unless we meet it head on with honesty and heal it, it will be a heavy burden we carry for many years. Guilt can be as heavy as lead.

In essence, the quote suggests that sometimes we don't fully comprehend the weight of our burdens until we experience the relief of their absence. Hester's journey from shame to freedom exemplifies this profound realization.

Living in Integrity: Honesty bridges the gap between our inner values and outer actions. It's easy to project a false image, but true integrity lies in aligning our behaviour with our beliefs. An honest life is a life of congruence.

So, let us practice Satya—speaking truthfully, acting authentically, and nurturing relationships built on trust. As we do, we pave the way for healthy, happy, and honest connections with ourselves and the world.

Story of – "Crystals and Chocolates: A Tale of Friendship and Faith"

A boy and a girl were friends who shared an interest in Buddhism. They often went to the local temple to learn the teachings of the Buddha and practice the Dharma. The boy had a collection of crystals that he had received from his grandfather. He valued them and used them for his meditation practices. The girl had a box of chocolates that she had bought from a festival, and she loved them as a special indulgence.

One day, the boy showed the girl his collection of crystals, and she was impressed by their color and shapes. In turn, the girl showed the boy her box of chocolates, and he was enticed by their aroma and taste. He was very economically poor, and his family could never afford a luxury such as chocolates.

The boy proposed that they exchange their belongings, as a sign of friendship and generosity. He said, "I will give you all my crystals if you give me all your chocolates". The girl agreed, as she thought that the crystals would help her recite the mantras.

The boy gave her all his crystals, but he secretly kept one, the most beautiful and meaningful of all, in his pocket. The girl kept her promise and gave him all her chocolates.

That night, the girl was happy with the exchange and slept peacefully in her bed, having sweet dreams.

However, the boy could not sleep, as he wondered if the girl had hidden some of her chocolates, just as he did with the crystal.

The next morning, the boy went to the girl and asked her, "Did you give me all your chocolates yesterday"? The girl replied, "Yes, I did. Why do you ask"? The boy said, "Because I did not give you all my crystals. I kept one, the most precious of all, in my pocket. I am sorry, I was greedy and dishonest. Please forgive me and take this crystal as well".

The girl smiled and said, "I knew that you kept one crystal, because I remembered the one that was your favorite. But I did not mind, because I also kept one chocolate, the most exquisite of all. I am sorry, I was also greedy and dishonest. Please forgive me and take this chocolate as well".

The boy and the girl realized their mistake and hugged each other. They returned each other's belongings and vowed to practice the Dharma more sincerely and faithfully.

Moral

If you do not give 100% in your relationships, you will always assume that your partner will not give 100% either. What you put into a relationship, is what you will receive. As the Bible says, what you sow, you will reap. If you want your relationships to be built on trust, you must be a participating factor in that.

Honesty grows your character. By being honest in relationships, you hold your partner accountable to do the same. It allows you and your partner to continually think about your choices and how it can help (or harm) your partner and your relationship.

"Being deeply loved by someone gives you strength while loving someone deeply gives you courage". — Lao Tzu

CHAPTER ELEVEN –
EVERYTHING BAD HAPPENS TO ME

Adversity is a universal experience; no individual passes through life without encountering challenges. The essence of our character is not defined by the adversities we face, but rather by our responses to them. Individuals with a pessimistic outlook tend to accept their fate without resistance, whereas those with an optimistic perspective view these challenges as opportunities for growth and learning.

It is essential to cultivate patience, for just as those who endure the rain are eventually greeted by sunshine, perseverance through difficult times leads to brighter days. Our beliefs shape our reality: if you are confident that things will work out, you will notice opportunities everywhere. Conversely, if you doubt the positive outcomes, your vision will be clouded by obstacles.

Just as storms shape skilled sailors, adversity strengthens us. Like trees buffeted by strong winds, we develop deep roots. But beware of shallow roots—those that make us unstable and prone to toppling. The stronger the winds, the stronger the wood.

Indoors, where wind is absent or minimal, trees may not experience the same forces that encourage deep root growth in nature. As a result, their roots may remain relatively shallow.

Botanists growing tall trees indoors, in malls and hotel atriums, struggle with this; often resorting to using fans to create artificial wind.

Rumi wrote, "What hurts you blesses you; darkness is your candle. These pains you feel are messengers. Listen to them". When faced with pain, consider it a messenger. Listen to its lesson. Treat every situation and person as a teacher. What are they trying to teach you today? This mindset is our antidote to defeat.

When Hernán Cortés, a Spanish explorer, arrived in Veracruz, Mexico in 1519, he started his ambitious campaign to conquer Central America. He commanded his men to destroy and set fire to their ships, so that they would not rebel or flee back to Cuba. Likewise, we sometimes need to eliminate our escape routes and cut off our ties, so that we can face our fears and advance in life into the unknown possibilities of our future.

When seemingly insurmountable obstacles arise, don't fold. Sharpen your blade and invent your way forward. The bolder, that was an obstacle for the weak, becomes a steppingstone in the path of the strong. Only by confronting our greatest fears do we discover our true strength.

Embracing the Fall: Lessons from Yoga and Life

In the serene space of a yoga class, where breath and movement intertwine, we find ourselves in asanas—those graceful yet challenging poses. It's here that we stumble, wobble, and sometimes fall. But in that fall lies a profound lesson: the art of rising stronger.

The Fall and Resilience: When we lose balance and topple out of an asana, we're not failing; we're learning. Each tumble becomes a stepping stone toward mastery. The person who falls and then rises—determined, unyielding—gains more than mere physical strength. They cultivate resilience, an inner fortitude that transcends the mat.

Fear as a Catalyst: Fear, in measured doses, can be transformative. It nudges us to confront our limits, to push beyond comfort zones. The fear of falling becomes the catalyst for growth. Sometimes we simply have to trust; jump and grow our wings on the way down. But chronic fear—the gnawing anxiety that never relents—saps our vitality. We must recognize when fear serves us and when it cripples us.

Healing Amidst Chaos: Life whirls around us, relentless and demanding. Amidst this chaos, we must carve out sanctuaries for healing. Our neurological well-being craves respite. If life doesn't offer it, we must create it. Chronic stress, left unchecked, morphs into anxiety—an insidious companion that shadows our steps. We owe ourselves moments of stillness, where the mind can mend. Inner stillness is our key to developing outer strength.

The Dance of Time: "I just don't have time", we tell ourselves. Yet, time is both finite and elastic. When we prioritize what truly matters—self-love, connection, growth, - the clock bends. We cease making time for trivialities, and suddenly, a window opens. Through that window, we glimpse self-love waiting patiently, beckoning us to step through.

In the grand theatre of existence, we are both the actors and the audience. Our falls, our fears, our stillness—they compose the symphony of our lives. So, let us embrace the fall, rise with grace, and dance to the rhythm of resilience.

Not everything we face can be changed, but nothing can change until we face it. Yoga teaches us to lean into the fear instead of away from it. Use it as an energy source to propel you instead of demobilizing you anchor holding you back.

The Story of - "The Wisdom of the Banyan Tree"

Once upon a time, in a serene monastery nestled amidst mist-covered mountains, there lived a young monk named Kavi. Kavi was known for his unwavering devotion to meditation and his deep understanding of the teachings of Buddha.

One stormy night, as monsoon rain lashed against the monastery's wooden walls, Kavi sat cross-legged in the meditation hall. The flickering candlelight danced on his serene face as he contemplated the nature of suffering. Outside, the ancient banyan tree stood tall, its gnarled roots gripping the earth like an old sage's fingers.

The abbot, venerable Master Baba Rama, entered the hall. His eyes, like polished onyx, held both compassion and wisdom. He approached Kavi, saw the fear in his eyes and said, "Young one, adversity is like the tempest that rages against the banyan tree. It tests our resolve, bends our spirit, and reveals our inner strength".

Kavi bowed respectfully. "Master Baba Rama, how can we transform adversity into wisdom"?

The abbot gestured toward the banyan tree. "Observe its roots, Kavi. They plunge deep into the soil, seeking nourishment and stability. The stronger the winds, the deeper the roots grow. But beware—the banyan also has aerial roots that dangle from its branches. These are shallow, seeking only easy paths to reach sunlight. They lack the strength to withstand storms".

Kavi gazed at the ancient tree. "And what does this teach us, Master"?

"Adversity is inevitable", Master Baba Rama replied. "No one escapes life unscathed. But it is not the adversity itself that defines us; it is our response. Negative minds accept fate passively, like the banyan's aerial roots. They sway with every breeze, unstable and easily uprooted".

"And positive minds"? Kavi asked.

"Positive minds", the abbot continued, "are like the banyan's deep roots. They embrace adversity, seeking growth and learning. Just as battles shape boys into men, adversity strengthens us. Our hearts become resilient; our minds unwavering".

"But what of pain, Master"? Kavi inquired. "How do we find solace"?

Master Baba Rama smiled. "Pain is a messenger, Kavi. Listen to its lesson. Treat every situation and person as a teacher. What can you learn from them today"?

Kavi nodded, absorbing the wisdom. "And when obstacles seem insurmountable"?

"Sharpen your sword and remove dullness, so you can cut deeper and change your circumstances", the abbot said. "Invent your way forward. Necessity births invention. Only by confronting our greatest fears do we discover our true strength. We never truly know how strong we are, until we face our greatest fear and have no choice but to conquer it".

From that day on, Kavi meditated under the banyan tree, its roots a reminder of resilience. When life's storms raged, he embraced them, knowing they were shaping his spirit. And when faced with pain, he listened—to the wind, to the rain, to the whispers of the banyan leaves.

And so, in the monastery's quietude, Kavi learned that adversity was not an enemy but a compassionate teacher. Just as the banyan's roots held firm, he anchored his heart in wisdom, and his spirit soared like the branches of the ancient tree.

May we all find strength in adversity, like the banyan tree with its deep roots and unwavering spirit.

The Story of – "We are the sky and not the clouds"

Imagine an airplane taking off and being immediately met with the challenge of navigating through a dense tapestry of stormy clouds. The once clear horizon is obscured by a tumultuous sea of grey, mirroring the cluttered state of an unsettled mind. Within the cocoon of the aircraft, visibility is reduced to a mere few feet beyond the windows, a metaphor for the limited perspective one often has amidst life's turbulence. The plane, like the practitioner of mindfulness, continues its steady climb, undeterred by the chaos that surrounds it.

Within the cockpit, the pilot's calm and focused demeanour serves as a beacon of stability. Each decision is made with mindfulness, each action a deliberate response to the present moment, unaffected by the storm's fury. This reflects the essence of mindfulness practice: the cultivation of an inner calm, a serene awareness that remains unshaken by the external storms of life. The passengers, entrusting their safety to the pilot, are reminded of the importance of trust — in themselves, in the process, and in the journey of life.

Then, almost as if by a miracle, the airplane pierces through the final layer of clouds, emerging into a realm of boundless blue skies. The sudden clarity and vastness of the open sky represent the mind's potential for peace and expansiveness when one navigates through the storms of thoughts and emotions with mindfulness. The sunlight, warm and enveloping, bathes everyone inside in a light of awakening, symbolizing the illumination that comes from deep understanding and clarity of mind.

This transition from storm to serenity mirrors the transformative journey of mindfulness. It is a vivid reminder that no matter the severity of the storm, the sky beyond is perpetually clear and serene. My father would often say, "This too shall pass. It may feel like a kidney stone, but it will pass".

The clouds of doubt, fear, and unrest are temporary obstacles on the path to inner peace. Just as the airplane continues its flight, trusting in its ability to reach clearer skies, so too must we keep moving forward on our mindfulness journey, knowing that tranquillity and clarity lie just beyond the clouds of our current troubles.

> "You are the sky. Everything else – it's just the weather".
>
> – Pema Chödrön

CHAPTER TWELVE –
TAKE THE PATH OF LEAST RESISTANCE

In the quiet chambers of retrospection, where the echoes of our past reverberate, we discover a profound truth: our most meaningful achievements in life were born from adversity. Like the lotus that blooms resplendently from murky waters, our journey toward purpose and fulfillment (our truth / dharma) often begins in the crucible of struggle.

Often the path of least resistance does not take you to the places in life with the most beautiful views as those are the more challenging paths. You have to usually work for the best scenic view, climbing over what seems impossible, being patient along the journey to not lose hope.

The person who insists on seeing with perfect clarity before they decide, never decides. To end in certainty, we must first begin with doubt. In the Tao it says, "The journey of a thousand miles begins with one step. The first step of any journey is the hardest, but step by step one travels far. To move a mountain, we must first begin moving a stone". The only impossible journey is the one that you never begin.

Buddhist wisdom teaches us that the path to enlightenment is strewn with challenges—each scar, each trial, a testament to our growth. These trials, though daunting, are the very chisels that shape our character. They carve resilience into our souls, etching a map of courage and tenacity. Our scars become sacred, for they remind us that transformation is not painless; it is the labor pains of rebirth.

Fear, paradoxically, becomes our thermometer. When our goals stir trepidation within us, we know we are on the right track. For aspirations that merely whisper comfort are but whispers of mediocrity. Dreams that ignite our hearts and haunt our nights—those are the ones that propel us beyond the mundane. They beckon us to ascend, to stretch our wings and soar toward the sun.

And so, we cling to our unseen roots—those hidden anchors that tether us to resilience. Just as a tree's roots delve deep into the earth, our inner strength burrows into the bedrock of our being. It sustains us as we climb the mountain of existence, step by arduous step. Happiness and understanding await us at the summit, bathed in the golden light of wisdom. Taking comfort in knowing that there is nothing more beautiful than a smile that has struggled through tears.

Once we reach the summit of any challenge that we face and we look back, we will realize that it was not the just mountain that we conquered, but more importantly our fears. Overcoming that negative self-talk in our minds telling us we are not good enough or that we are underserving of success. Our potential is only limited by our imagination, but so often held back by our fears.

In the grand fabric of life, our scars are not blemishes; they are the threads that weave our story. Celebrate them, for they are the alchemical gold that transforms suffering into purpose. As we ascend, let us honor our resilience—the quiet hero that whispers, "You are enough, you deserve this".

The Story of - "Bamboo's Rooted Resilience"

Bamboo, often hailed as the fastest-growing biomass on our planet, harbors a secret. But let's not be too hasty in our assumptions.

Bamboo, that elegant grass, doesn't bloom frequently. It's a patient soul, requiring 65 to 120 years of existence before it even considers flowering. Yet, when it does, it orchestrates a symphony of survival. In a phenomenon known as gregarious flowering, bamboo bursts forth with seeds simultaneously, even if separated by a hundred miles. This synchronized spectacle overwhelms predators, ensuring that some seeds find fertile ground to sprout and thrive.

Now, let's shift our gaze to the Chinese Bamboo Tree. Its growth story is a masterclass in patience and resilience. Picture this: in the first year after planting its seed, there's no visible sign of activity. The second year? Still nothing. The third- and fourth-years pass, and the soil remains undisturbed. Our patience wavers; doubts creep in. Are our efforts in vain?

But then, in the fifth year, behold—a miracle unfolds. Growth erupts, and it's no ordinary growth. The Chinese Bamboo Tree shoots up 80 feet in a mere six weeks! Imagine witnessing a 36-inch surge in just 24 hours. You can almost set your watch by its upward march, ticking away at a pace of up to 1.6 inches per hour.

Now, here's the twist: Did the Chinese Bamboo Tree slumber for four years, only to explode into exponential growth in the fifth? Not quite. Beneath the surface, hidden from our impatient eyes, it was busy crafting a robust root system—a foundation strong enough to bear the weight of its towering aspirations.

And so, it is with people. Life's shortcuts? Mere illusions. There's no mystical elevator to success, no express route to enlightenment. Instead, we climb a twisting, spiraling staircase—each step a lesson, each turn an opportunity.

When we look back, we realize that anything worthwhile that we have accomplished in our lives, had originally scarred us and challenged us. If your goals don't frighten you just a little, then most likely you are aiming too low. Our resilience, like those unseen roots, sustains us as we ascend toward happiness and understanding.

Remember this: Rooted resilience is our true companion on this remarkable journey.

CHAPTER THIRTEEN –
YOU CAN NEVER HAVE ENOUGH

In our fast-paced modern lives, it seems we're perpetually chasing more—more success, more possessions, more experiences. Yet, amidst this relentless pursuit, we often forget to pause and appreciate what we already have. Yoga, with its ancient wisdom, gently awakens us; reminding us that "enough" is a powerful word and one that transcends material accumulation.

Consider the blessings we hold: the warmth of sunlight on our skin, the laughter of loved ones, the simple pleasure of a shared meal. These are the threads that weave the structure of our existence. When we shift our focus from what's lacking to what's abundant, we begin to discern the essential from the frivolous.

The Australian Aboriginal people express this beautifully: "We are all visitors to this time, this place. We are just passing through. We are here to observe, to learn, to grow, to love, and then we return home". Life unfolds swiftly, like a fleeting breeze. Amidst this rush, we must intentionally slow down—to savor the taste of each moment, to marvel at the intricate details of existence.

Yet, how often do we find ourselves physically present but mentally absent? Our bodies move through the day's tasks, while our minds race ahead, perpetually in "got to go" mode. In this haste, we overlook the everyday miracles—the delicate bloom of a flower by our driveway, the kaleidoscope of colors in a sunset, the gentle touch of raindrops on a windowpane.

Yoga traces its roots to the tantric tradition, which invites us to engage all our senses fully. It whispers that God speaks to us in subtleties—a rustling leaf, a fleeting smile, a dew-kissed morning. But our inner chatter, like a noisy stream, often drowns out these whispers. We miss the magic woven into our surroundings—the symphony of birdsong, the texture of tree bark, the wonder in a child's eyes.

Next time you rush to work, pause. Notice the fragile flower that unfurled just for you. Lift your gaze to the sky; let the sunset's hues imprint on your soul. Feel the breeze kiss your cheeks and meet the curious gaze of a child at the grocery checkout. These are the ephemeral gifts—the poetry of existence—that vanish when our minds wander elsewhere.

Morning Gratitude: A Simple Practice with Profound Impact

Each morning, as consciousness gently embraces me, I engage in a tiny meditation of gratitude. Before my eyes fully open, before I reach for my phone or step out of bed, I pause and ask myself, "What am I grateful for today"? It's a quiet dialogue with my soul—a moment to acknowledge the blessings that weave through my existence.

The beauty lies in its simplicity. Every day unfolds uniquely. Sometimes, it's the grandeur—the power of a thunderstorm, or the warmth of a loved one's touch. Other times, it is the seemingly trivial—the aroma of fresh coffee brewing, the softness of my pillow, or the way sunlight dances on the floor.

Why do I begin my day this way? Because gratitude is my compass. It orients me toward the heart of life, where joy resides. And I invite you to join me on this journey.

I would ask that give this a try for two weeks—just a handful of moments each morning. Observe how it transforms not only your day's beginning but also your perception of reality. As you cultivate gratitude, you become a magnet for more blessings. Life responds to your openness, composing magic into the ordinary.

Our existence is a canvas painted with miracles—the dew dripping off a flower's petals, the playful sound of a morning bird, the whispered secrets of wind blowing through leaves. Yet, we often rush past, chasing tomorrows. Let us pause. Let us slow down, open our senses wide, and drink in the beauty that surrounds us.

The future beckons, but today is a gift—an exquisite tapestry of fleeting moments. Don't miss it. For within the ordinary lies the extraordinary, waiting to be seen.

The Story of - "The Simple Life: The Greek Fisherman"

A businessman was on a short vacation in Santorini, a small Greek island. He couldn't sleep, so he decided to walk along the pier. He saw a small boat with a single fisherman inside. The boat was filled with several very large yellowfin tuna.

"Wow, those are impressive fish. How long did it take you to catch them"? he asked the fisherman.

"Not long at all", the fisherman replied.

"Then why don't you stay out longer and catch more"? the businessman suggested.

"I have enough for my family and some friends", the fisherman said, as he loaded the tuna to a wheeled cart.

"But what do you do with the rest of your time"? the businessman wondered.

The fisherman smiled and said, "I enjoy my life. I sleep late, fish a little, play with my children, take a nap with my wife, and walk to the village in the evening, where I drink wine and play guitar with my friends".

The businessman laughed and said, "Sir, I am an investment banker from New York. I have an MBA from Harvard and I can help you. You should fish more and sell the extra fish. With the money, you could buy a bigger boat and catch even more fish. Soon, you could have a fleet of fishing boats and sell your fish directly to the customers. We call this vertical integration; you could control the whole business, from production to distribution. You would have to move to Athens, of course, to manage your growing empire".

The fisherman asked, "But, sir, how long would all this take"?

"About 10 to 15 years, maybe 20 at most", the businessman said.

"And then what"? the fisherman asked.

The businessman smiled and said, "That's the best part. When the time is right, you could go public and sell your company shares to the market and become very rich. You would make millions".

"Millions? And then what"? the fisherman asked.

The businessman said, "Then you could retire and move to a small coastal fishing village, where you could sleep late, fish a little, play with your kids, take a nap with your wife, and walk to the village in the evening, where you could drink wine and play guitar with your friends".

CHAPTER FORTEEN –
KEEP YOUR EYE ON THE PRIZE

"While goals serve their purpose, in our modern lives, we often become overly fixated on achieving them. We create to-do lists, diligently ticking off tasks, all the while missing the essence of the journey itself. Happiness lies not solely in reaching the destination, but in the steps we take along the way.

In the teachings of the Tao, Lao Tzu wisely said, "A good traveler has no fixed plans, and is not intent on arriving". This reminds us to embrace the unfolding path, rather than clinging to rigid plans. Paths are created by walking and not by waiting and planning.

Interestingly, it's often the most challenging segments of our journey that offer the most breathtaking views. Amelia Earhart aptly stated, "Adventure is worthwhile in itself". So, even when we feel adrift, unable to discern our exact path, remember that paths reveal themselves as we walk.

Wandering doesn't equate to being lost; it signifies openness to discovery and the beauty of the unknown.

The Story of - "The Lotus Seeker"

In a town nestled amidst the mist-covered mountains, there lived a young monk named Kavi. Kavi was known for his gentle spirit and unwavering devotion to the teachings of the Buddha. His days were spent in quiet meditation, seeking answers to life's profound questions.

One crisp morning, Kavi decided to embark on a pilgrimage. He yearned to visit the sacred temple atop the highest peak—the place where the ancient scriptures whispered secrets of enlightenment. The journey was arduous, but Kavi's heart burned with purpose.

As he ascended the rugged trails, Kavi encountered fellow travelers. Some were seasoned pilgrims, their faces etched with wisdom. Others were wanderers—nomadic souls seeking solace. Kavi listened to their stories, shared his meager provisions, and offered kind words. He understood that each traveler had their own path, their own quest for meaning.

One day, Kavi met an old woman named Sita. Her eyes held a lifetime of sorrows, and her steps faltered. She clutched a tattered map, its ink faded by time. "Young monk", she said, "I seek the Lotus Lake—a place said to hold healing waters. Can you guide me"?

Kavi studied the map. Its lines zigzagged, leading nowhere in particular. "Sita", he said, "the true path lies within. The Lotus Lake is not a distant oasis; it resides in your heart. Seek stillness, and you shall find it".

Sita frowned. "But the map…"

Kavi smiled. "Not all who wander are lost. Sometimes, the wandering itself is the pilgrimage. Let go of the map and let your heart guide you".

Sita hesitated, then folded the map and placed it in her worn satchel. Together, they continued their journey. Kavi shared stories of compassion, of the lotus blooming from murky waters. Sita listened, her steps growing lighter.

At last, they reached the temple. Its golden spires touched the sky, and the air hummed with ancient chants. Kavi bowed before the altar, feeling the presence of countless seekers who had come before him. Sita stood beside him, tears streaming down her weathered cheeks.

"Is this the Lotus Lake"? Sita whispered.

Kavi shook his head. "No, my dear friend. The temple is but a reflection. The true Lotus Lake lies within, where compassion meets wisdom. It is the stillness that blooms even amidst chaos".

Sita closed her eyes. In that sacred space, she found solace. The lotus blossomed within her—a fragile yet resilient flower. She no longer needed the map; her heart had become her guiding light.

As Kavi descended the mountain, he realized that enlightenment wasn't confined to lofty peaks. It was in the kindness he showed, the stories he heard, and the shared laughter. Not all who wandered were lost; they were simply on different paths, seeking their own lotus within.

And so, Kavi continued to wander, knowing that the journey itself was the destination. For in the wandering, he discovered the truth: "The secret to having it all is knowing you already do".

May your own journey be filled with wisdom, compassion, and the blossoming of your inner lotus.

CHAPTER FIFTEEN –
SOME BONDS ARE TOO STRONG TO BREAK

Our lives are woven together by the threads of daily habits and rituals. These patterns, however, are often shaped by the conditioned delusions of our human minds. We find ourselves influenced by the illusions propagated by society, media, education, and politics—each trying to impose its views and agendas upon us. In this dance of conformity, we tend to follow blindly, rarely questioning or examining the validity of these narratives.

Buddhism, with its ancient wisdom, invites us to awaken from this state of ignorance and confusion. It beckons us to be more than mere reflections of others—to become lamps unto ourselves. Imagine breaking free from the chains of collective delusion, forging our own path, link by deliberate link.

In his book The Christmas Carol, Charles Dickens wrote, "I wear the chain I forged in life", replied the Ghost. "I made it link by link and yard by yard; I put it on of my own free will, and of my own free will I wore it. Is its pattern strange to you"? Indeed, we forge our own shackles, whether consciously or unwittingly, and bear them with the same sense of purpose.

There are moments when we feel trapped by our own actions and habits, as if they exist beyond our control. Yet, hidden within this perceived helplessness lies a profound truth: choice. We always have the choice to change, to liberate ourselves. Our innate wisdom and compassion can guide us through the labyrinth of suffering—our own and that of others.

The Buddha's words echo across time: "No one saves us but ourselves. No one can, and no one may. We ourselves must walk the path". This is the essence of freedom and responsibility. We hold the brush that paints our reality; we decide what we see and how we respond. So, my friend, may you glimpse the path to freedom in your life—a path illuminated by your own inner lamp and not blindly following the light of others.

The Story of - "How to train an elephant"

In the quietude of the forest, where ancient trees whisper their wisdom, there exists a tale—a parable woven into the very fabric of existence. It speaks of an elephant, not merely flesh and bone, but a vessel for deeper truths.

They lead the baby elephant, wide-eyed and curious, into an empty tent—a sanctuary of shadows. There, they drive an iron stake into the earth, its formidable length reaching toward the heavens. Ten feet of unwavering resolve, anchored deep within the soil. The air hums with anticipation as they unfurl a chain—thick, unyielding, and cold as forgotten memories.

They attach the chain to one foot of the baby elephant. As is always the case when force is applied, the opposite reaction is resistance. Its wild spirit flares, a tempest of defiance. It strains against the chain, the tiny feet scraping against the weight of fate. But the links hold firm, and the stake remains unyielding. The earth itself seems to whisper, "Stay, little one. You are bound".

Days stretch into years, and the elephant is now fully grown. Its once-tiny frame now commands space, muscles rippling beneath its hide. Yet, the restraint remains—a mere thread of rope now, compared to the iron chain that once imprisoned it. A thin rope, almost translucent, connects the beast to a modest wooden peg. The elephant could snap it with a thought, a flicker of intention.

Why, then, does it stay? Why does it not stride forth, break free, and reclaim its birthright—the vast expanse of the forest, the distant mountains, the horizon that beckons?

The answer lies in conditioned memory—the echo of a time when the world was smaller, when the chain was unbreakable. The young elephant, with eyes wide as moons, had fought and lost. It learned the language of captivity, etching the lie into its very brain: "You cannot escape".

And so, the mighty creature stands, tethered by a fragile thread. It feels the rope's presence, a phantom weight. But it does not test its strength. It does not shake its leg and watch the rope slip away. Instead, it remains—a prisoner of its own history, a captive of belief.

We, too, carry our ropes—the stories we tell ourselves, the whispered doubts that bind us. We were once small, vulnerable, and we believed the stakes were immovable. Now, as adults, we wear the invisible threads—the "cant's" and "shouldn't"—and we forget that we possess the strength to break them.

But listen closely. The forest murmurs secrets. The wind carries echoes of liberation. The Buddha himself, under the Bodhi tree, understood this truth: We are not bound by iron or rope; we are bound by our minds.

So, my friend, let us remember our wildness—the untamed spirit that knows no chains. Let us shake the dust from our memories and step beyond the wooden pegs of doubt. For we are not elephants; we are seekers of truth, wanderers of possibility. And the vastness of existence awaits those who dare to believe: "I have what it takes".

Ask yourself, "What chains do I wear in life of my own making". Give yourself permission to release yourself from captivity back into the wild. May your footsteps be free, and may your heart know its wings.

CHAPTER SIXTEEN – ONLY THE STRONG SURVIVE

While the narrative of evolution often emphasizes survival of the strongest and fittest, scientific evidence reveals that true survivability lies not only in physical prowess, but also in the capacity to hold onto hope and adapt to changing circumstances.

Hope, like an anchor on a weathered boat, doesn't shield us from life's tempests. Instead, it steadies our vessel amidst the raging waves. Let us explore this metaphor:

The Anchoring Force: Imagine a small boat adrift in a stormy sea. The anchor plunges into the depths, its iron teeth gripping the ocean floor. Similarly, hope digs into our soul, providing stability when life's gales threaten to capsize us. It doesn't prevent storms; it anchors our resolve.

Storms Will Come: Storms—those inevitable trials—sweep across our existence. They arrive unbidden, tearing at our sails, drenching us in uncertainty. Yet, hope whispers, "This too shall pass". It doesn't halt the tempest; it nurtures our endurance.

The Dance of Waves and Anchor: The anchor doesn't fight the waves; it surrenders to their force. Likewise, hope doesn't deny adversity; it embraces it. It says, "Hold fast, for storms are transient". Hope doesn't promise smooth seas; it promises resilience.

Waiting for the Calm: As the boat rocks, the anchor holds firm. It doesn't rush the storm's departure; it patiently waits. Similarly, hope doesn't demand instant relief; it sustains us through the squalls. It reminds us that even in chaos, there's an underlying order.

Beyond Survival: Hope isn't survival alone; it's thriving. The anchor doesn't merely prevent drift; it allows the boat to rest, repair, and prepare for fairer winds. Likewise, hope isn't passive endurance; it's the promise of renewal.

So, when life's tempests rage, remember your inner anchor—the unwavering hope that holds you steady. It won't stop the storms, but it will keep you afloat until the sun breaks through the clouds.

The story of - "The Three Psychiatrists"

In the heart of Vienna, during the tumultuous period leading up to World War II, three Jewish psychiatrists found themselves entwined in the intricate fabric of human existence. Each held a unique lens through which they perceived the human psyche, and their perspectives were as diverse as the colors of a mandala.

Sigmund Freud, the venerable intellectual, had delved into the depths of our minds, unraveling the enigma of our desires. His wisdom whispered that pleasure was the primal force propelling us forward—the sweet nectar that fueled our actions and shaped our lives.

Alfred Adler, the second master, stood on a different precipice. His gaze pierced beyond the veil of pleasure, revealing a hidden truth. To Adler, the heartbeat of humanity pulsed with the rhythm of power. We all danced to the primal beat of asserting control, yearning to rise above our perceived inferiority, and etch our significance upon the canvas of existence.

And then there was Victor Frankl, the fledgling psychiatrist, eager to tread the path blazed by his mentors. But destiny wove a cruel web. As the storm clouds of World War II gathered, the Nazis cast their ominous shadow. Freud and Adler, luminaries of the field, fled the impending darkness. But Frankl's footsteps faltered, and he found himself ensnared— a prisoner in a Nazi concentration camp for four harrowing years.

Within those barbed-wire confines, Frankl witnessed a paradox. The robust withered, having their strength consumed by suffering, while the seemingly frail clung to life, with tenacity. Why? What force sustained them through this inferno?

Frankl pondered, transcending Freud's pleasure principle. Pleasure was a distant echo in that desolate Concentration Camp. Instead, he glimpsed a flicker of something deeper—a spark that defied despair. It wasn't pleasure; it was meaning. The fragile souls found purpose in their suffering, a reason to endure. They clung to threads of hope, weaving meaning into their existence, even amidst the abyss.

In the crucible of anguish, Frankl discovered a truth that transcended pleasure and power: meaning—the silent companion that whispered courage to the weak, resilience to the broken, and purpose to the lost. And so, against all odds, they held on, not for pleasure, but for the sacred flame of meaning, hope burned within.

In the annals of psychiatry, these three—Freud, Adler, and Frankl—etched their stories. One sought pleasure, another grasped for power, but the third, oh, the third sought meaning. And in that pursuit, he found a philosophy that echoed across the ages—a philosophy rooted not in hedonism or dominance, but in the quiet nobility of purpose.

Viktor E. Frankl, penned the profound and enduring work titled "Man's Search for Meaning". In this poignant memoir, Frankl chronicles his harrowing experiences during World War II, where he grappled with suffering, loss, and the extent of human cruelty. But within those desolate confines, he unearthed a beacon of hope—a psychotherapeutic method that transcended despair.

Frankl's approach, known as logotherapy, sought to illuminate the path toward meaning. He believed that purpose was the beacon navigating us through life's darkest storms. Three avenues led to this elusive meaning: completing tasks, caring for others, or facing suffering with unwavering dignity.

Amidst the barbed wire and shadows, Frankl observed a paradox: those who clung to a purpose—imagined conversations with loved ones, whispered dreams of tomorrow—defied the odds of survival. Their inner flame burned brighter than the cruelty that engulfed them. While the strongest and fittest would not survive.

He found that hope was the last emotion to die in a human. Without hope, people would succumb to the cruel fate of the camps. However, those with a reason to live somehow found a way to survive.

In the annals of human thought, "Man's Search for Meaning" stands as a testament to resilience, a hymn to the human spirit. It whispers across generations, reminding us that even in suffering, life pulses with significance.

May we, too, find our meaning, our North Star, as we navigate the labyrinth of existence.

CHAPTER SEVENTEEN –
BEAUTY FADES BUT DUMB IS FOREVER

While the allure of physical beauty may wane over time, our intellect possesses an inherent resilience. Consider this: if we focus solely on external appearances, we may perceive beauty as fleeting. Yet, the realm of intelligence transcends such transience.

Modern science delves into the intricate workings of our brains, unraveling their mysteries. **Neuroplasticity**—the brain's remarkable ability to rewire itself—stands as a testament to our cognitive adaptability. Traumatic brain injuries, once thought to be insurmountable, yield to diligent therapies and tenacity.

Our minds, akin to fertile soil, thrive on nourishment. What we feed them shapes our mental health and intellect. Education becomes the beacon that dispels the shadows of ignorance.

Eckhart Tolle wrote, "Where there is anger, there is always pain underneath". In the wisdom of Buddhism, the dichotomy of "good" and "evil" dissolves. Instead, we encounter a simpler truth: knowledge versus ignorance. When someone inflicts pain upon us, a yogi's heart expands. They recognize it as an act born not of malice, but of ignorance—an ignorance that blinds the doer to the ripples of suffering they create.

So, if life presents challenges, remember this: education holds the key. Within each of us lies untapped potential, akin to the young Thomas Edison in the tale below. Just as he harnessed his brilliance, so too can we unlock our latent capacities.

As the founder of Ashtanga Yoga, Pattabhi Jois, whispered to his disciples, "Do your practice, and all shall unfold". Let these words echo through your being, for wisdom blooms not in the petals of a fading flower, but in the luminous core of understanding.

The Story of - "Thomas Edison and Our Potential"

At a tender age, Thomas Edison returned home from school, clutching a sealed envelope. His teacher had entrusted him with a message meant solely for his mother. With anticipation, he handed it to her.

As Nancy, Edison's mother, unfolded and read the note, her eyes welled up with tears. "What does it say, Mother"? Edison asked, his heart racing. Nancy took a deep breath and read aloud: "Your son is a genius. This school is too confining for his brilliance, lacking the caliber of teachers needed to nurture his talents. Please take charge of his education".

And so she did. Nancy became both teacher and mentor, guiding her son through uncharted territories. Little did they know that this pivotal decision would shape history. Thomas Edison, against all odds, emerged as one of the greatest inventors of the century.

Years later, after Nancy's passing, Edison sifted through old family belongings. In a forgotten corner of a desk drawer, he discovered a folded paper. As he unfolded it, the words etched upon it struck him like lightning: "Your son suffers from severe learning disabilities and mental deficiencies. We regretfully expel him from our school".

Edison wept, his tears a testament to the resilience of the human spirit. In his diary, he penned these words: "Thomas Alva Edison, once deemed mentally deficient, transformed into the genius of the century—a transformation fueled by the unwavering love and determination of a heroic mother".

CHAPTER EIGHTTEEN –
IT IS BETTER TO RECEIVE THAN GIVE

A successful relationship requires balance and mutual effort. My dad, who has been married to my mom now for 65 years, always told me: "A relationship only works if both people put in the same honest effort". He compared it to a horse drawn carriage. "The horses need to pull their weight equally. Otherwise, the carriage will go nowhere and only around in circles".

However, some people end up in unbalanced relationships. This can happen with your work, your friends, or your partner.

A parasitic relationship is one in which one person consistently takes more from someone else than they give back. When we face this situation, we have a choice to make. We can either ask them to give back equally, accept this behavior fully or end the relationship.

I have witnessed many patients who struggle to get over a failed relationship. For many, I find that they started the relationship with imbalance, and it was doomed to fail. Their retirement plan was sadly to find a rich partner to take care of them. That never works out well. When the taker's only asset, such as physical attractiveness, fades, the relationship collapses.

A beautiful face will age and a perfect body will change, but a beautiful soul will always be a beautiful soul. If they want to save the relationship, they must give back as much as they receive. I try hard to teach, especially women in my life, to become fiercely independent.

Others are on the opposite side of the equation. They give until they have nothing left. They lose their affection and respect for their partner. They build up resentments that turn toxic. They need to remember that they are in charge of their own destiny.

An old Native American proverb says: "You can't wake up someone pretending to be asleep". This means you can't change others if they don't want to change. Before you try to change others, just remember how hard it is to change yourself. You cannot teach someone something they think they already know. The only person you can change is yourself.

With wisdom, we learn what we need and what we need to let go. Which bridges to cross and which we need to burn. Some people are not meant to stay in our lives. Some changes are not what we want, but what we need for our mental health. Sometimes, walking away is the best way to move forward.

Jack Canfield wrote, "If you surround yourself with people who are strong and positive, you are much more likely to see a world of opportunity and adventure". Life is precious. Cherish the people who broaden your horizons, bring you joy, and love you unconditionally. Surround yourself with those who uplift you, not those who just take and drag you down.

The Story of – "The Two Seas"

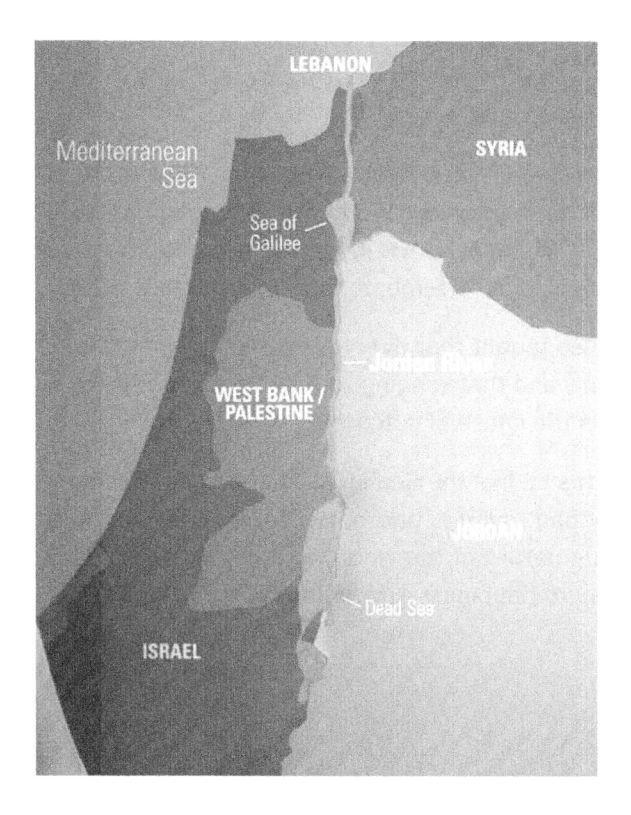

In the land of Israel, there are two bodies of water that receive water from the same source, the Jordan River. One is the Sea of Galilee, a sparkling lake full of fish and abundant life, surrounded by greenery and flowers. It is a place of beauty and joy, where people come to fish, swim, and relax. The other is the Dead Sea, a vast pool of salt and minerals. It is a place of desolation and decay, where nothing survives for long.

What makes these two seas so different when they both receive water from the same river? The answer is simple: the Sea of Galilee gives as much as it takes, while the Dead Sea only takes and never gives. The Sea of Galilee lets the water flow through it, nourishing the land and the life around it. The Dead Sea hoards the water, keeping it for itself, until it evaporates and becomes bitter and poisonous.

These two seas are like two kinds of people in the world: those who are generous and those who are greedy. Those who are generous share what they have with others, and in return they receive happiness and peace. Those who are greedy cling to what they have, and in return they suffer from dissatisfaction and misery.

This is the teaching of the Buddha, who said: "Giving brings happiness at every stage of its expression. We experience joy in forming the intention to be generous. We experience joy in the actual act of giving something. And we experience joy in remembering the fact that we have given".

The Buddha also taught that everything in this world is impermanent and interdependent, and that clinging to anything as if it were permanent and independent is the cause of suffering.

Therefore, let us be like the Sea of Galilee, and not like the Dead Sea. Let us give freely and joyfully, and not cling selfishly and miserably. Let us realize the true nature of the world, and not be deceived by its illusions. This is the way to happiness and liberation.

CHAPTER NINETEEN –
IF WE DON'T LIKE THE ANSWER, ASK ANOTHER QUESTION

Some people say that prayer is a way of asking for some intervention or giving thanks, but meditation is a way of listening. Rumi wrote, "There is a voice in us that has no words, listen".

It does not matter if you believe in a higher power or not. It does not matter what your faith or religious creed is. When you meditate, you quiet your mind and let your soul speak. Is this the voice of God or something else? That is up to you to decide.

But sometimes we don't like what we hear. Sometimes we cling to our expectations and hopes; we ignore the reality that awaits us. Sometimes we miss the opportunities that are right in front of us, because we are too busy chasing the ones that never existed.

The Story of – "God often gives us answers, but we want to listen on our own terms"

Paul was a devout man who trusted God with all his heart. He lived in a valley near a dam. One morning, the dam burst, and the valley started to flood.

A neighbor drove up to his house and shouted, "Paul, hurry up! The dam broke and the whole valley is flooding. Come with me now…"

Paul replied, "Thank you, but I have faith in God. He will take care of me and protect me. You go ahead".

The water level rose, and the house began to fill with water. Another neighbor came by in a boat and said, "Paul, come quickly. Your house is about to submerge under the water. You have to leave now!"

Paul said, "Thank you, but I have faith in God. He will take care of me and protect me. You go ahead".

Soon, the water covered the house and Paul had to climb to the roof, where he sat and prayed. A Coast Guard helicopter flew over and saw Paul. They said over the speaker, "Sir, we are here to rescue you. We are going to lower a basket and lift you to safety".

Paul said, "Thank you, but I have faith in God. He will take care of me and protect me. You go ahead".

In a few more minutes, the water engulfed the house and Paul drowned. When he reached Heaven, he saw God and said, "What happened, God? I had faith that you would protect me and keep me safe. How did you let me die"?

God said, "Paul, what more could I have done? I first sent you a car, then a boat, and finally a helicopter!"

The story of Paul and the flood illustrates the importance of faith and practice. Faith (saddhā, śraddhā) is a serene commitment to the teachings of mindfulness and to the enlightened beings, such as Buddhas or bodhisattvas. A bodhisattva is a person who is on the path to becoming an enlightened being but is still her to help others. Practice is the concrete actions we engage in based on faith, such as meditation, ethical conduct, and compassionate service.

Paul had faith in God, but he did not practice his faith. He did not heed the warnings of his neighbors, who were sent by God to rescue him. He did not take action to save himself or others from the flood. He did not realize that God's help came in various forms, and that he had to cooperate with God's will. He was attached to his own idea of how God should save him, and he rejected the reality of the situation. He was passive, arrogant, and ignorant.

Buddhism teaches that faith and practice are inseparable and interdependent. Faith inspires us to practice, and practice deepens our faith. Faith alone is not enough; we also need to apply our faith in our daily lives and use our wisdom and compassion to deal with the challenges we face.

Practice alone is not enough; we also need to have faith in the Dharma teachings, and trust in the guidance of enlightened beings. Faith and practice are the two wings of a bird that enable us to fly to the state of buddhahood, the ultimate goal of Buddhism.

The moral of the story is that we should not rely on faith alone, but also on practice. We should not be complacent, but proactive. We should not be stubborn, but flexible. We should not be blind, but aware. We should not be foolish, but wise. We should not be selfish, but altruistic. We should not be deluded, but enlightened. We should not be like Paul, but like the Buddha.

CHAPTER TWENTY –
THE ONLY WAY TO STOP CHANGE IS TO RESIST IT

Transformation is a journey that we all must go through in life. It is not always easy, nor pleasant. It can be lonely, messy, difficult, and painful. But it can also be beautiful, rewarding, enlightening, and liberating.

Transformation is the process of letting go of what no longer serves us, and embracing what helps us grow. It is the process of shedding our old self and emerging as our new self. It is the journey of letting our ego fade away and the emergence of our true nature.

Yoga is a powerful tool for transformation. It helps us connect with our body, mind, and spirit. It helps us balance our energy, calm our emotions, and clear our thoughts. It helps us align with our purpose, values, and goals. It helps us cultivate awareness, compassion, and wisdom.

Transformation is not a linear or predictable process. It is a dynamic and creative process. It involves cycles of change, challenge, and growth. It involves moments of crisis, confusion, and doubt. It involves moments of breakthrough, clarity, and confidence.

Transformation requires courage and resilience. It requires us to face our fears, overcome our obstacles, and embrace our opportunities. It requires us to accept our reality, adapt to our circumstances, and act on our potential. It requires us to be honest and open.

Transformation is not something that happens to us, but something that happens within us. It is not something that we can control, but something that we can influence. It is not something that we can avoid, but something that we can welcome.

Transformation is a natural and inevitable process. It is a part of life, and a part of us. It is a gift, and a responsibility. It is a challenge, and an opportunity. It is a journey, and a destination.

The Story of - "Personal Transformation"

As you breathe deeply and relax your body, imagine that you are a caterpillar wandering through the Forest of Loving Awareness. You are curious and joyful, exploring the beauty of nature and feeling the warmth of the sun. You have everything that you need, and you are content with your life.

But one day, you sense a strange and powerful force inside you. It feels like a pressure that is pushing you to change. You are afraid and confused, and you try to resist this force. But the more you resist, the more pain you feel. You wonder what is happening to you and why.

You hear a voice in your heart, telling you to trust the process and surrender to the flow. You feel a primal urge to find a safe place, where you can prepare for something unknown. You climb up a branch, spin a silken thread and hang upside down. Then you wait.

You enter a state of deep meditation, where you let go of your thoughts and emotions. You focus on your breath and your inner light. You feel a connection with the source of all life, the universal energy that flows through everything.

As you meditate, your body begins to transform. You shed your caterpillar skin and a hard-shell forms around you. You are enclosed in a dark and tight chrysalis, similar to a cocoon. You feel isolated and lonely, and you wonder if you will ever see the light again.

You remember the voice in your heart, telling you to trust the process and surrender to the flow. You realize that this is a necessary stage of your growth, and that you are not alone. You are supported by the universal energy, and by all the beings who have gone through this before. You are part of a larger cycle of life, death and rebirth.

You feel a new wave of strength and courage from within, that you have never felt before. You feel ready to break free from the chrysalis and embrace your new self. You push against the shell and crack it open. You emerge as a beautiful butterfly, with colorful wings and a radiant glow. You discover that strength does not come from doing what you can do, it comes from overcoming what you first thought was impossible.

You feel a sense of awe and gratitude, as you see the world from a new perspective. You see the Forest of Loving Awareness in a new light, full of wonder and magic. You feel a connection with all living things, and a compassion for their suffering. You realize that you have a purpose and a mission, to spread love and joy wherever you go.

You hear the voice in your heart, telling you to trust the process and surrender to the flow. You understand that this is the essence of the Buddhist philosophy, and the path to enlightenment. You are a butterfly, and you are free.

The Story of – "The Leaf on the Stream of Consciousness"

In a village cradled by the embrace of whispering forests and tranquil mountains, lived Tenzin, a monk whose wisdom was as vast as the skies above. His insights into the nature of joy and sorrow were sought after far and wide, making him a beacon of enlightenment in a world of shifting shadows.

Enter Maya, a young seeker burdened with the oscillating tides of her emotions, who approached Tenzin with a heavy heart. "Master Tenzin," she implored, "my heart rides on crests of euphoria only to plummet into valleys of despair. How can I anchor myself amidst these tumultuous waters"?

Tenzin led Maya to a babbling brook, where the dance of water over stone whispered ancient secrets. He selected a leaf that had fallen in silent sacrifice and laid it upon the stream. "Observe this leaf as it journeys with the water," he guided her.

As Maya watched, the leaf glided with grace, now twirling in a playful vortex, now surging forward with the stream's eager rush. Maya listened intently as Tenzin continued, "The leaf does not resist the water's flow. It does not cling to the calm nor despair in the rapids. It simply allows the stream to guide its journey, knowing that each twist and turn is part of its path."

"Behold the leaf," Tenzin stated, "our happiness, too, waxes and wanes, mirroring the infinite cycle of the seasons. There are times when joy buoys us high, and we feel untouchable. Yet, there come moments when sadness ensnares us, and we fight to surface".

"In the same vein," he continued, "when joy fills you, let it overflow, illuminating the path for others. And when sorrow comes calling, welcome it, for it is but a traveler passing through. Remember, after every storm, the sun will shine; such is the way of happiness".

With eyes now open to the wisdom of Tenzin's words, Maya watched the leaf disappear from view. A serene calm enveloped her.

"Thank you, Master Tenzin," she expressed, her smile a reflection of newfound peace. "I grasp now that happiness, like the seasons, is ever-changing yet always returning. I will cherish each moment, be it under the sun or clouds, knowing that both sculpt the journey of life".

Thus, Maya ventured forth, her spirit lightened, carrying the eternal cycle of joy and sorrow with grace, spreading the sage words of Tenzin to every seeking soul she met.

CHAPTER TWENTY ONE - IT IS NOT MY FAULT

In discovering happiness through mindfulness, taking ownership of one's life is a cornerstone. This profound concept transcends mere acceptance of circumstances; it involves a deep acknowledgment that our happiness and unhappiness are largely products of our perceptions, reactions, and internal narratives.

By embracing responsibility for our emotional states, we liberate ourselves from the often fruitless endeavor of assigning blame to external factors or individuals for our discontent. This shift in perspective is not about fault-finding within ourselves but about recognizing our power to influence our own well-being.

Central to this empowerment is the notion of "owning your breath," a metaphor for taking control of the one thing in life that is truly ours: our response to the world around us. Breath, in its simplicity and constancy, is a tool for grounding and centering, offering a pathway to inner peace regardless of external chaos.

When we own our breath, we cultivate a space within ourselves that is untouchable by external circumstances. No one can steal our happiness or disturb our peace of mind without our implicit permission. Over time we value this harmony so much, that anything that threatens to take away this inner peace, simply becomes too expensive. This realization is liberating, offering a sense of serenity that is both profound and enduring.

The practice of mindfulness, rooted in Buddhist teachings, guides us to live in the present moment, fully and without reservation. This practice illuminates the transient nature of emotions and thoughts, revealing that our essence remains untouched by the fleeting dramas of life. By cultivating an awareness of the present, we learn to navigate the ebb and flow of emotions without becoming ensnared.

This awareness allows us to experience life's complexities without losing our foundational peace and happiness. It teaches us that while we cannot control every aspect of our external environment, we can master our responses to it, thus owning our emotional landscape. It allows us space to slow down, think rationally, and not to make long term decisions based on short term problems.

Embracing ownership of our happiness requires a compassionate, non-judgmental approach towards ourselves and others. It encourages us to view our journey through a lens of growth and understanding rather than criticism and blame. This path of ownership and mindfulness fosters a deep, abiding happiness that is not contingent on the actions or approval of others but is rooted in our own inner strength and wisdom. By integrating these practices into our lives, we embark on a transformative journey toward sustained happiness and peace, guided by the timeless wisdom of Buddhist principles.

While slipping into the role of a "victim" might seem easier, offering a temporary solace in the face of adversity, it ultimately leads to a sense of powerlessness and stagnation. On the other hand, embracing ownership of one's feelings and circumstances paves the way for genuine empowerment. This proactive stance encourages individuals to recognize their capacity for change, fostering resilience and personal growth.

Taking responsibility for one's emotional state and life conditions is not about blaming oneself for misfortunes but about reclaiming control over the narrative of one's life. It shifts the focus from external forces to internal strength, opening up pathways to healing, transformation, and ultimately, a more fulfilling life experience. This empowerment through ownership ignites a profound transformation, turning obstacles into opportunities for growth and self-discovery.

The Story of – "There's a Hole in MY Sidewalk"

"I walk down the street.

There is a deep hole in the sidewalk.

I fall in.

I am lost... I am helpless.

It isn't my fault.

It takes forever to find a way out.

I walk down the same street.

There is a deep hole in the sidewalk.

I pretend I don't see it.

I fall in again.

I can't believe I am in the same place.

But, it isn't my fault.

It still takes me a long time to get out.

I walk down the same street.

There is a deep hole in the sidewalk.

I see it is there.

I still fall in. It's a habit.

My eyes are open.

I know where I am.

It is my fault. I get out immediately.

I walk down the same street.

There is a deep hole in the sidewalk.

I walk around it.

I walk down another street".

— Portia Nelson, There's a Hole in My Sidewalk: The Romance of Self-Discovery

This story serves as a powerful metaphor for the journey towards mindfulness, highlighting the process of becoming aware of one's patterns, acknowledging the freedom of choice in steering away from repetitive negative circumstances, and ultimately embracing responsibility for one's actions to forge a more positive life trajectory.

CHAPTER TWENTY TWO -
THE BEATINGS WILL CONTINUE UNTIL MORAL IMPROVES

The exact origin of the phrase is not well-documented. It has been variously attributed to seafaring practices, military leaders, and harsh corporate environments, but these attributions are anecdotal and not supported by solid evidence.

The saying is a part of a larger family of sayings that emerged around the mid-20th century and has been found in various forms in military and naval publications, humor columns, and satirical pieces. It reflects a long-standing theme of satirical commentary on the absurdities of authority, particularly when that authority is blind to the welfare and morale of its subordinates.

The saying has been used in various forms over the years, such as "layoffs will continue until morale improves" and "there will be no liberty on board this ship until morale improves," reflecting a widespread recognition of the absurdity of trying to enforce morale through punitive measures.

In the journey of mindfulness, leadership transcends traditional boundaries of authority, blossoming into an inspiring force guided by wisdom and compassion. Whether within the intimacy of our homes or the complexity of the workplace, the essence of our motivational approach profoundly shapes collective values and productivity.

In this enlightened age, the antiquated notion encapsulated by "The beatings will continue until moral improves", stands in stark contrast to the principles of a modern society. Reflecting on tales like Mutiny on the Bounty, while such tactics may have temporarily served figures like Captain Bligh, ultimately, they proved unsustainable and detrimental.

The ancient Roman sage, Publilius Syrus, captured the essence of enlightened leadership with his observation, "You can accomplish by kindness what you cannot by force". This enduring insight highlights the transformative power of motivation when it is rooted in compassion and empathy. By nurturing an atmosphere of respect and positive reinforcement, leaders can ignite a genuine passion and commitment within their teams or families.

Echoing this sentiment, Lao Tzu's wisdom, "Those who flow as life flows know they need no other force," illuminates the core of mindful leadership. Authentic leaders eschew coercion in favor of harmony and alignment with life's natural rhythms. This gentle guidance encourages individuals to discover their unique paths and contribute with authenticity.

Albert Einstein, renowned for his contributions to physics and philosophy, articulated the ineffectiveness of force in achieving peace: "Peace cannot be kept by force; it can only be achieved by understanding". This principle is profoundly relevant in leadership, where true harmony emerges from a foundation of mutual respect and empathy. Striving to comprehend the perspectives and needs of those we lead fosters an environment ripe for collaboration and forward movement.

The Tao Te Ching offers a timeless lesson: "Gain entry not by force or will but only by softness". This sage advice underlines the effectiveness of gentle persuasion and empathy in overcoming challenges. Leaders who embrace this philosophy can transcend resistance, paving the way for authentic engagement and collective growth.

The Tao further teaches us, "Water is fluid, soft, and yielding. But water will wear away rock, which is rigid and cannot yield". This illustrates the subtle power of gentleness and adaptability. By embodying these qualities, leaders can steer through challenges with grace and resilience, setting a powerful example for others to follow.

Whenever we attempt to impose our will, whether it be in mechanical endeavors, personal relationships, or professional settings, we are often met with resistance. This is a natural reaction to the force applied. On the other hand, adopting a gentle and empathetic approach to motivation might require more time and effort initially, but it yields far more enduring and positive outcomes compared to the results achieved through force.

The Story of – "The Gentle Shall outlast the strong"

In the heart of the ancient kingdom of Dhammapada, there lived a ruler named King Suryaketu. His reign began with great ambition and a firm hand, guided by the belief that strength and authority were the pillars of effective leadership. Suryaketu, much like the leaders of old, adhered to the principle that "The beatings will continue until moral improves," a mantra that echoed through the halls of his palace and across his lands. Yet, despite his power and the fear he inspired, his kingdom was fraught with unrest, his people disheartened, and his court filled with silent dissent.

One moonlit evening, as Suryaketu wandered the palace gardens, he stumbled upon an elderly monk, Vimala, meditating under the ancient Bodhi tree. Intrigued by the monk's serene presence, Suryaketu approached him. Vimala opened his eyes, and with a gentle smile, invited the king to sit beside him. The king, moved by an inexplicable sense of peace, shared his burdens and the challenges of his reign.

Vimala listened intently, then spoke softly, "O King, your strength has built walls, but kindness builds bridges. Your efforts, rooted in force, have sown seeds of resistance. But through compassion and empathy, you can nurture a garden of trust and loyalty".

These words struck a chord in Suryaketu's heart. The king realized that his rigid control had disrupted the natural harmony of his kingdom, much like a stone disturbing the calm waters of a pond.

Vimala explained that lasting peace could not be kept by brute force, but could only be achieved by understanding. King Suryaketu understood that true peace and prosperity in his kingdom could only arise from mutual respect and empathy. Water embodies fluidity, softness, and adaptability. Yet, it has the power to erode even the toughest rock, which remains inflexible and unyielding. With his kindness, he could carve out canyons.

Inspired by these lessons, King Suryaketu embarked on a transformative journey. He replaced his forceful decrees with open dialogues, listening to the needs and perspectives of his people. He embraced the ethos of mindful leadership, recognizing that true authority comes from inspiring and guiding with wisdom and compassion. Slowly, the kingdom transformed. The people, once disheartened, now flourished under his gentle rule. Productivity and happiness blossomed like never before, proving that kindness and understanding wield the true power to change the world.

King Suryaketu's legacy became a testament to the enduring wisdom of mindfulness and compassion in leadership. His story, passed down through generations, served as a beacon of hope and a guide for leaders everywhere, teaching that the strength of a kingdom lies not in the might of its ruler, but in the hearts of its people, united by a leader who walks with them, in gentleness and empathy, toward a brighter future.

Groupthink Bias

Leadership, in its most effective form, thrives on diversity of thought and open dialogue. However, when leaders succumb to "Groupthink Bias", the repercussions on decision-making can be significantly detrimental.

Groupthink occurs when the desire for harmony or conformity within a group result in an irrational or dysfunctional decision-making outcome. It is particularly prevalent in environments where dissent is discouraged, and consensus is valued above all else. This phenomenon often leads to poor decisions, as critical analysis and alternative viewpoints are sidelined in favor of unanimity.

Oppressive leaders exacerbate this issue by surrounding themselves with "yes people," individuals who, out of fear or desire for favor, refrain from offering honest feedback or challenging the leader's ideas. This creates an echo chamber where the only voices heard are those echoing the leader's opinions, effectively silencing dissent and critical thinking. The consequences of such leadership are many, leading not only to flawed decision-making but also to an organizational culture that stifles innovation and discourages the healthy exchange of ideas.

The classic tale of "The Emperor's New Clothes" by Hans Christian Andersen serves as a poignant illustration of these concepts. In this story, an emperor, obsessed with his appearance and clothes, is deceived by two swindlers who promise him a suit of clothes invisible to those who are unfit for their positions or "hopelessly stupid". Out of fear of being perceived as inadequate or unintelligent, everyone, including the emperor, pretends to see the magnificent clothes. It isn't until a child, unaffected by the pressures of conformity and fear of retribution, truthfully exclaims that the emperor is wearing nothing at all, that the spell of groupthink is broken. This narrative highlights the dangers of leadership that values appearance and conformity over truth and integrity. It demonstrates how an environment that does not encourage honest feedback is doomed to folly and embarrassment.

This story and the broader implications of groupthink serve as a cautionary reminder of the importance of fostering a culture of open communication and critical analysis within any leadership structure at home and at work. Leaders must actively seek diverse perspectives and encourage constructive dissent to avoid the pitfalls of groupthink. Only by embracing the courage to confront uncomfortable truths and challenge prevailing assumptions can leaders make well-informed decisions and lead their organizations toward sustainable success.

THE EPILOGUE

Well, this takes us to the end of this stage of our journey together. It marks only the beginning of the next step on your life's journey. I hope our time together has been enlightening and contributed to your pursuit of happiness.

Embarking on this journey is often simpler than seeing it through to its end; hence, prepare as if you're setting out on a lengthy voyage. Embrace each day as if it were your last, yet cultivate knowledge with the belief that you will live forever.

Whenever you find your spirit waning, allow this book to help you refill the fuel back into your lamp of wisdom, reilluminating your inner light. The Buddha said, "If you follow the light of your heart, you will never get lost and you will always find your way home".

The story of your life is yours to write, and as you wield the pen now, remember, there are no short cuts to any places truly worth visiting. Embrace the labor, assume responsibility, and transform your existence into a courageous odyssey.

Life is like a book you can't just put down. You must read every word, every scene, every person. Some parts will bore you; some parts will break you. You will face things you'd rather avoid; you will fall in love with things you can't hold on to. What's meant for you will find you. But you must keep reading. Stories give your life meaning and purpose. Live your story, don't let it pass you by, but instead allow it to unfold like a beautiful flower.

Every choice you make can steer you to a completely different destination. Echoing the Buddha's wisdom, "You are always at a new beginning". It's never too late to navigate your life towards positivity, regardless of age or past decisions.

Forgive yourself for the times you lingered longer than necessary where you shouldn't have. For the times you caught yourself, going back to the same place that made you sick, expecting to feel better. The optimal time to start a change was perhaps in the distant past, but the second-best moment is now. Embrace the uniqueness of the present, for you will never come this way again.

It is never too late to turn on the light. You can break any bad habit or stop any negative thought, regardless of how long they have been with you; you can change your outlook, no matter how long you have held on to the old one. When you flip the switch, it doesn't matter how long the darkness has been there. The light still fills the room and chases away the shadows, letting you see what you couldn't see before.

Looking back a year from now, you will celebrate the bravery you showed in making today's changes. Own your breath, nurture peace within your mind, fortify your body, and let your heart overflow with love.

In the words of Ram Das, "We are just walking each other home".

THANK YOU FOR SHARING THIS JOURNEY WITH ME.

Please stay in touch: www.energyyoga.com

@DAVID_YGLESIAS

@ENERGY_YOGA

MINDFULNESS COURSES AND YOGA TEACHER TRAINING

Explore the path to becoming a Yoga Alliance Certified Instructor with David Scott Yglesias, or delve deeper into mindfulness and enhance your yoga practice through our Online University. For more information, visit: energyyoga.thinkific.com/collections.

Energy Yoga Online university presents a flexible learning approach to suit your needs, offering courses in three formats: entirely online, a hybrid of in-person and online sessions, or completely in-person. We also offer an Affiliate Programs. If you own your own yoga studio and offer teacher training, you can partner with us and use any of our modules for your program for a shared revenue.

- 200 Hour Yoga Alliance Teacher Training
- 300 Hour Yoga Alliance Teacher Training
- The Art of Vinyasa Sequencing
- Anatomy, Physiology and Mental Health

ABOUT THE AUTHOR
David Scott Yglesias

David Scott Yglesias, a native of South Florida, has always felt a deep connection to the water. Whether diving into the ocean depths or gracefully paddleboarding across serene mangrove lagoons, saltwater courses through his veins. But David's journey extends far beyond the sea.

In 2006, he founded the Energy Yoga & Wellness Center in Doral, Florida, a sanctuary where mind, body, and spirit converge. With over 10,000 hours of practical teaching experience, David has guided countless students through transformative yoga and meditation classes. His passion lies in sharing the ancient wisdom of yoga with a modern Buddhist twist.

As an E-RYT-500 registered with the Yoga Alliance, David not only teaches but also leads yoga teacher trainings. His impact reaches across continents—from bustling cities in China to the lush rainforests of South America. Through his guidance, aspiring teachers find their voice and purpose, spreading the light of yoga worldwide.

Beyond the mat, David wears multiple hats. He is a licensed Massage Therapist and a Kinesiologist, blending science and holistic healing. Yet, perhaps most importantly, he is a devoted student of mindfulness. David strives to live by its code—cultivating presence, compassion, and gratitude in every moment.

Thank you for joining David Scott Yglesias on this mindful journey, where the bustling modern world converges with serene soulful introspection of ancient knowledge.

Printed in Great Britain
by Amazon